RIMFIRE RIFLES

A BUYER'S AND SHOOTER'S GUIDE

by

STEVE MARKWITH

Part of the *Survival Guns* series of books
published by:

Prepper Press
Your Survival Library

PrepperPress.com/SurvivalGuns

ISBN 13: 978-1-939473-30-1

Printed in the United States of America.

Prepper Press Paperback Edition: September 2015

Prepper Press is a division of Kennebec Publishing, LLC

Special thanks to Pyramyd Air for their cooperation in lending photographs to help complete this book.

ABOUT THE AUTHOR

Steve has a lifelong interest in just about all things that shoot including rifles, shotguns, revolvers, pistols, airguns, and black powder guns, as well as vertical or horizontal bows. He began formal firearms training at age 11 during NRA-sanctioned small-bore target rifle events, and was an active hunter by the age of 12. He began reloading shotgun shells at 14, using a handheld Lee Loader to feed his addiction. After joining the U.S. Army, he served two combat tours in Vietnam, gaining experience with numerous military firearms during Air Cavalry helicopter operations and ground-based reconnaissance missions.

Upon returning to civilian life, Steve resumed shooting, participating in NRA bullseye, combat pistol, and trap events. These activities expanded his reloading experience to metallic ammunition and bullet casting. Steve eventually became an NRA-certified pistol, rifle & shotgun instructor, as well as a certifying official for state firearms permit applicants. He also worked for a well-known gunsmith and PO Ackley disciple, until an untimely death forced a career change.

Joining a major state correctional agency, Steve was soon appointed as a firearms instructor, eventually assuming control of all state correctional firearms operations. He's still working, and holds a master instructor rating, plus numerous other federal, state, and industry certifications. He has over 25 years of full-time firearms training experience, and many industry connections.

Steve also has extensive hunting experience in the Northeast, and at other locations throughout the United States. He holds an archery deer record, and actively remains afield on a year-round basis, whether chasing spring turkeys or winter coyotes with night-vision equipped AR-15s. He also writes when time permits, and has had numerous articles published about firearms and the great outdoors.

PREFACE

Several years ago, a friend called up with an agricultural problem. Her vegetable garden was being devoured by a very large woodchuck bent on the total elimination of any remaining green beans. The large, furry rodent had been at it a while, so the odds of a winter vegetable supply were rapidly decreasing. Meanwhile, her granola-eating neighbor considered this varmint to be a cute and cuddly pet. The question was, could I make the problem disappear quietly?

Well, as it turned out, I could. A few days later, I sat on her porch while sipping ice tea, approximately twenty-five yards above the garden. The downrange area was uninhabited, so the main concern was noise. Before long, Ol' Chuck appeared, clearly in the mood for beans. Instead, he got a .22 Short through his noggin, compliments of a simple rimfire single-shot rifle. The report was almost nonexistent, but the results were decisive, and nobody was the wiser. In fact, the loudest sound was probably the firing pin striking the cartridge. The bullet made an audible "thump", but that was

There's more to rimfires than the "twenty-two". These woodchucks were "pasteurized" by a brace of .17 Hornady Magnum Rimfire rifles.

about it. I carefully pocketed the spent casing. The green-bean-eating groundhog was moved to an undisclosed location, and life returned to normal. The technology that made this possible was about as basic as one could get.

Woodchucks are edible, as are many other species that could be quietly harvested in a pinch. Many, like squirrels or cottontail rabbits, are smaller and less tenacious. As quiet as that .22 Short was, there are even less noisy, lower-powered choices. With all the recent hoopla surrounding so-called silencers, it's worth noting that clandestine shooting is possible for no more investment than an inexpensive box of .22 CB Caps, which will provide airgun-like performance for less than six bucks.

Some potential table fare will require a harder-hitting round, but by simply switching loads, one can advance up the .22 caliber power ladder. In fact, by choosing a more potent rimfire caliber, significant performance gains can be realized. It really boils down to a full understanding of the entire rimfire spectrum. Knowledge is king.

THE SURVIVAL GUNS FIREARMS SERIES

This book is one of several *Survival Guns* firearm publications. The first book lays out some basic principles, and the others deal with specific firearm systems. A "system" consists not only of a gun, but also its ammunition and related equipment. An in-depth examination of each system will permit full exploitation of its capabilities. Planned procurement can provide a useful collection of mutually supportive firearms capable of covering our needs. Some basic tenets govern the process, and the series runs as follows:

Survival Guns: A Beginner's Guide: In the first publication we laid out some groundwork for a practical collection of firearms. Each was chosen from key requirements. Widespread use, dependability, ease of operation, and availability of parts, accessories, and ammunition were thrown in the mix. Also covered was a hard look at firearms safety and responsible firearms ownership. Part of that process involved secure storage methods. We procured a gun safe and then framed up a small but practical inventory of firearms based on these requirements, adding a shotgun, rimfire rifle, centerfire rifle, and a handgun. The idea was to choose, when possible, types with similar function. Use of each would thus promote skills with another to improve overall proficiency. Towards that goal, our initial selections were based on the K.I.S.S. principle. We had to start *somewhere,* and most of us don't have deep enough pockets to rush headlong into the nearest Guns-R-Us for an arm load of shootin' irons. We needed something to cover the basics while developing resources to fund other items. That's where the second book began...

Shotguns: A Comprehensive Guide: This title served as a specific firearms starting point, and examined this versatile but often misunderstood firearm. You'll sometimes hear it called a "scattergun" in reference to its multiple-projectile payload. However, pellet distribution is based on a number of factors ranging from gauges through chokes. In a pinch, we can also utilize single projectiles to extend our range or tackle big game. Once understood, the shotgun affords some useful options, making it a great first choice for our safe. It also makes a great foundation for future acquisitions, which leads us to the next edition.

Airguns: A Buyer's and Shooter's Guide: Air-powered guns offer many useful possibilities for informed shooters. First, we can mail order both airguns and their ammunition, which don't fall under the jurisdiction of BATF (check your local regulations). Airguns also tend to be quiet - a useful advantage if low-impact hunting is necessary. The right choice will have adequate power for small game, and possibly even deer. From here it gets better since uninformed people will lump them all together as simple BB guns. In fact, airguns still maintain social acceptance not only domestically, but also around the globe. As a result, sophisticated designs have evolved with outstanding performance. Some are even sold in head-turning calibers like 9mm, .45, or .50-caliber! On a smaller and more affordable scale, we can also improve our all-around shooting skills while having some low-cost fun. Since an understanding of the various power-plants is essential, this guide will provide the necessary information for its purchase and use.

Rimfire Rifles: A Buyer's and Shooter's Guide: This book is devoted to a whole series of useful firearms, beginning with the well-known .22 Long Rifle. The venerable "twenty-two" hosts a wide array of interesting loads, including some ultra-quiet choices and fairly nasty high-speed rounds. Even hotter rimfire calibers include the .22 Winchester Magnum Rimfire, plus three small-bore derivatives: the .17 Mach II, .17 Hornady Rimfire Magnum, and Winchester's high velocity .17 Super Magnum. Careful shopping can provide us with a useful rimfire (or maybe even two) with which to quietly harvest small game or eliminate pests. An economical .22 LR firearm can also serve as a great high-powered rifle trainer if similar function is considered. In a pinch, it might even work for self-defense. The rimfires can't do everything, but they can do a lot once fully understood. One trait is easy to overlook until you start shooting. They're lots of fun!

Before getting started, we should consider the guidelines that govern all system choices.

SELECTION GUIDELINES

Several key requirements were identified in the previous editions. With apologies to those readers who already labored through them, the following criteria may avoid some future headaches:

Whatever we're looking at must be in widespread use: In the case of a rimfire rifle, one might substitute "must" for "should". If a primary firearm (such as a defensive shotgun) breaks, we're vulnerable until repairs can be made. If a small game-getting .22 quits, it may not be as big a crisis. Still, an established design is reassuring. It takes time for a system to gain recognition and grow in numbers. Well-established firearms have plenty of history behind them, and will hold few surprises. Widespread use is an indicator of numerous desirable traits.

Whatever we choose should be something with a solid reputation for dependability: It's comforting to have confidence in a chosen tool. As explained in *Survival Guns*, there are teething pains with many new products, and firearms are no exception. It's not uncommon to run into issues, ranging from function through ergonomics. Anecdotal experience based on one or two examples can give you a false read, and more often than not, seems to be the basis for unswerving opinions. A well-established track record is the better bet.

It must be easy to operate: Disparate function is never a good thing during stressful circumstances, and operational proficiency is commensurate with training. The more complicated something is, the more training will be necessary. If time and range access are issues, simple is better. Since we may be using our rimfire as a surrogate trainer for other systems, it's worth thinking on a larger scale. Also, simpler designs normally offer less opportunity for breakage. But even the simplest systems can quit working at some point, so…

Parts must be readily available: There are piles of .22 rifles in disuse due to seemingly minor problems like lost magazines. During the *Shotgun Manual*, we held up the Remington Model 870 as an example of 10 million-plus firearms that have been in continuous production since 1950. In other words, plenty of spare parts abound. The same is true of Ruger's popular 10/22 rifle. After more than half a century, it's still selling like hotcakes. There are other types as well, like Marlin's line of .22 semi-autos, bolt-actions, and leverguns. Using a proven system, you can predict which parts are likely to fail and stock up on spares.

Ammunition must be widely available: Until very recently, just about any hardware store with an FFL had a few boxes of .22 Long Rifle on hand. Your uncle or buddy might still have some, but nowadays, .22s are nearly as scarce as chicken lips, even though some manufacturers are cranking out one million rounds per day! Obviously, much of it is being stashed. It finally appears as if things are improving, although costs have risen somewhat. Regardless, the .22 LR is still relatively affordable when compared to most centerfire cartridges. It's also a universal load, unlike the recent but obscure .17 Mach 2. When you're buying, mainstream choices are just about always cheaper. If you're scrounging, the odds will tip in your favor. You can also benefit from a much wider selection of loads to match individual requirements.

It must be easy to maintain: Since no firearm is truly weatherproof, it should be serviced after exposure to the corrosive effects of snow, rain, or salt water. Easy disassembly really helps, and also promotes regular mainte-

The ubiquitous .22 is not only popular, but also diverse.

nance. In this case, we're talking about field servicing, rather than complete parts removal. Rimfires like the .22 LR produce a dense accumulation of fouling over time. Without cleaning, even the best-designed models will quit at some point. Simpler designs facilitate the process, which will also prolong the life of your investment.

It should accommodate practical accessories: It's easy to overlook some simple necessities, one good example being a sling. QD sling swivel mounts help, whether offered from the factory or fitted later. Scope mounts are important, too. By sticking with the most popular guns, availability of such accessories is assured. Once again, the Ruger 10/22 shines as such an example. Replacement barrels, stocks, bolts, and triggers can all be user installed without special tools. Informed consumers can select a gun capable of adapting to those upgrades they deem necessary.

It must represent good value: The well-known rule of thumb is to buy the best equipment you can afford. However, when it comes to firearms, "equipment" means more than just a gun. Looking at a rifle, some basic extras like a scope, mounts, sling, case, ammo, and a few spare magazines may be needed. Adding up the essentials creates a figure constituting the real bottom line. We call this our "system cost". To stay within our means, some budgeting may be required, so an honest gun at a fair price helps keep a lid on costs.

Especially in the case of rimfires, there are plenty of great rifles to choose from. Most gun stores and many big-box retailers will have *something* in stock. A *good* final choice can be daunting, but by keeping the above principles in mind, we can narrow down the field. A basic understanding of the various designs can help sort things out.

TABLE OF CONTENTS

CHAPTER 1

INTRODUCTION

For a book devoted to small caliber guns, it's somewhat strange to concede that the first slot in any gun safe should be occupied by something different. Those starting from scratch will need a do-all firearm, and a 12-gauge shotgun is a very good starting point. There is little that can't be done with this versatile system and the right assortment of shells. It's a formidable deterrent that can also handle the largest animals, along with small game and waterfowl. Who could possibly need more? Well, me for starters!

A couple of drawbacks are a shotgun's somewhat limited range, and noise. The range concerns can be addressed with a rifle more potent than a rimfire (this topic will be thoroughly examined in a future *Survival Guns* firearms edition). The noise concern may be a crucial problem in some circumstances, one that is best solved with a quiet rimfire rifle or possibly an airgun. Sure, you could screw a silencer on your AR-15, assuming you have the finances and fortitude to undergo the process. However, a suppressed .223/5.56 still sounds about as loud as a .22 Magnum, which could be purchased with a supply of ammo for less than the cost of just the muzzle device.

As for foraging, a number of animate targets can effectively serve as supper. Most of the smaller and more abundant species will be shredded from a hit with a high-velocity rifle bullet. How about a handgun? Well, truthfully, most people are lousy shots with one: good enough to hit a man-sized silhouette at very close range, but not a squirrel at 20 yards. Plus, even a .22 pistol is fairly loud with *any* type of ammo. Suddenly, the small-bore rifle options become viable choices. By far the most popular is a garden-variety .22 caliber, which makes a great choice for small game while providing an affordable means to practice marksmanship.

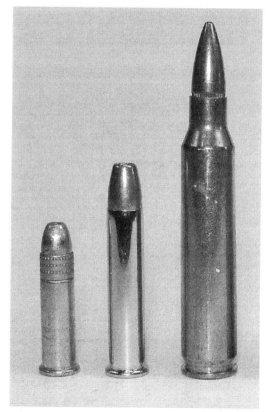

The 22 Long Rifle and .22 Magnum are a whole lot quieter than the .223/5.56 (R).

Low cost, low recoil, and low noise are among the twenty-two's primary attributes.

That said, a rimfire rifle of any type is no toy! In a pinch, although not recommended as a first choice, it could also be employed for self-defense. You can also stash a large quantity of ammunition in a very small area. And speaking of ammo, a huge selection is available, including some lesser-known types that offer nearly silent shooting. Perhaps the biggest thing of all is the easiest one to miss: a .22 is just plain fun!

For a modest investment, one can acquire a rifle, a few accessories, and a supply of ammunition. From that point on, odds are good that your larder can be stocked with small game. If things totally tank, while the mall crowd is desperately trying to figure out how to eat their makeup, a properly equipped person can rustle up a tasty dinner of gray squirrels (which, incidentally, do taste like chicken).

I'm a proponent of firearms with similar function. A carefully chosen .22 offers a great opportunity for some economical training through a concept some refer to as an "understudy gun". You may have already seen such an example within *Survival Guns: A Beginner's Guide*. It contains a chart showing three pump guns: a shotgun, the rimfire, and a centerfire rifle. While none represent the zenith of firearms design, they do share the desirable trait of similar function.

When viewed in this context, a low price tag is not necessarily the top priority. Many people seem aghast at the thought of spending no more than is absolutely required for a firearm that is "only a twenty-two". One amazing virtue of this caliber is that you still can obtain a fully serviceable rifle for around one hundred bucks. It might be a well-worn single-shot bolt-action dating to the 1950s, but odds are, if the bore is okay, it'll shoot pretty darned well.

If viewed from a training perspective, an initial rimfire investment may be offset by ammo savings. I enjoy shooting an S&W AR-22, not only because it's an absolute hoot, but also because it works exactly like a centerfire AR-15. The same principle applies nicely to other action types. Two boxes (100 rounds) of .22 LR can provide plenty of practice. Since you'll also be enjoying the experience, the good

Centerfire AR-15 (top) and rimfire Smith & Wesson M&P-22 companion.

news is that you can keep shooting without going broke.

When discussing .22 LR, the abbreviation refers to "long rifle", the most common of several twenty-two caliber versions. Nowadays, the long-rifle offering is so universally popular that many folks may not recognize its older siblings. These include the .22 Long and .22 Short, among others. We'll thoroughly examine the choices, including some recent and more potent rimfire versions.

The 5mm Remington Magnum Rimfire, .22 Magnum Rimfire, .17 Mach II, 17 Hornady Rimfire Magnum, and .17 Winchester Super Magnum make our list. They boost performance by increasing velocity, which flattens trajectory to extend useful range. Each caliber shares the .22 rimfire's aptly named ignition system, whereby the rim is struck to detonate an annular deposit of priming compound. This old and simple design still works well with lower-intensity ammunition, and helps keep a lid on cost.

Before delving into the latest high-performance derivatives, let's wrap our arms around the famous double-deuce. Although you can spend a large pile of cash on one, for the most part, a twenty-two really is the "everyman's rifle". This statement transcends not only gender, but age. Many of us have fond memories of our first gun, and five will get you ten it was a .22. I still remember mine, presented at the ripe old age of eleven years – a Mossberg single-shot Model 320 K bolt-action. Since then, I've gone through a pile of twenty-twos. Truthfully, recommending one specific model isn't easy, especially if viewed in a systems-based context. A complete examination of all available rifles would require a full-blown book. Instead, I'll throw in comments pertaining to models with which I have experience.

A good source for information is Rimfire Central (www.RimfireCentral.com). You'll find threads related to models, ammunition and gear. Although it's always wise to take Internet information with a grain of salt, you can discover trends through multiple posts.

CHAPTER 2

RIMFIRE RIFLES - A FIRST LOOK

Rimfire rifles have been in continuous production for approximately a century and a half. The passage of time has presented ample opportunity for the development of numerous designs. Although some unusual types have appeared, we're better served by sticking with the mainstream choices. Long-standing popularity affords ample time for refinement of the various systems and emergence of some winning models. What follows is an examination of the prevalent designs.

COMMON RIMFIRE ACTIONS

Many guns, including rimfire rifles, operate off of common action themes. An "action" classifies the mechanical process used to feed, fire, extract, and eject cartridges. The associated parts are located in a primary housing, commonly referred to as a "receiver". The stock, magazine, and barrel connect to the receiver. The rear (or breech) end of the barrel contains a chamber, which is a slightly enlarged section of the bore, closely cut to match the dimensions of a cartridge. A rifle designed to

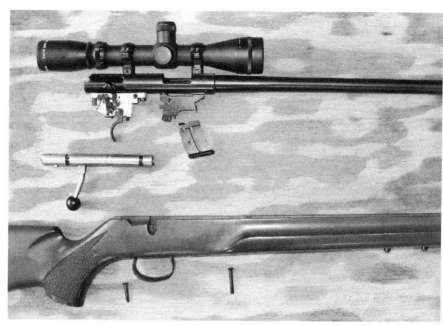

The main components of a bolt-action .22 rifle.

fire .22 Magnum cartridges will be "chambered" for this ammunition, and its barrel will be stamped accordingly.

Most but not all popular action types employ a reciprocating "bolt", which cycles ammunition through the action. The bolt is powered by one of several means described below. It contains a firing pin and extractor. Once fully locked forward against the chamber end of the barrel (or breech), the bolt and expanding cartridge case will safely contain the substantial pressure developed during ignition of a cartridge. This force will not only expel a bullet, but in the case of a semi-automatic design, it may also be used to power the action. A bolt-mounted claw can then grasp the rim of a fired casing, extracting it from the barrel's chamber. As the bolt travels rearward, the rim will contact an ejector, flinging it free of the action. Assuming the rifle is of a repeating design, the return of the bolt will feed and chamber another cartridge from a magazine.

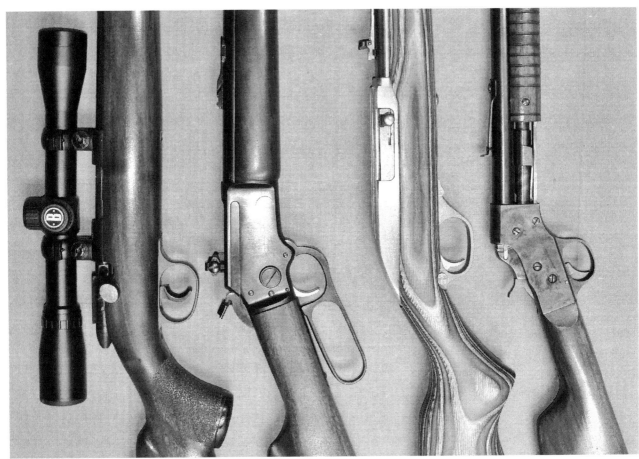

Common rimfire actions (I-R): bolt, lever, semi-auto, and slide-action.

Bolt-actions: Rifles in this category employ a manually operated handle. The shooter grasps a knob to cycle the reciprocating bolt, which is typically housed within a tubular receiver. As explained above, the bolt contains a firing pin and extractor. Working it cocks the action, chambers cartridges, and then ejects them. The process is well-developed and simple, meaning that it's easy to use. Rifles may be single-shots or repeaters that feed from detachable or tubular magazines. Just about all can be used as single-shots if cartridges are manually fed to their chambers. This feature can come in handy when firing specialty rounds like quiet CB Caps, which behave as low-powered .22 Shorts. A bolt-action is also fundamentally strong, making it a logical design for hotter calibers like a .22 Magnum.

Semi-automatics: You'll sometimes see such firearms described as auto-loaders or "self-loading". Recoil force is harnessed to drive the bolt rearward, cocking the rifle while initiating extraction and ejection. A recoil spring undergoes compression, which then imparts energy to return the bolt and feed a new round. Although it's easy to burn through a pile of ammo, each shot still requires a separate pull of the trigger (a true "automatic" or machine gun will continue to fire as long as the trigger is held rearward). Proper function is dependent on a balance of recoil and spring force. For this reason, most designs require ammunition that develops the requisite energy. Most, but not all, will be limited to .22 Long Rifle cartridges.

Slide actions: Otherwise known as "pumps", these rifles employ a reciprocating forend that connects to the bolt by a linkage. Function is not too different from a semi-auto, but the shooter imparts the force needed for cycling. Pump guns have been around for well over a century, but popularity has gradually waned due to the proliferation of reliable self-loaders. While just a few models remain, the design still has merit. Besides offering function similar to a slide action shotgun, the rimfire versions aren't finicky about ammo. They normally run off tubular magazines which hold copious quantities of .22s. If you can drop in some cartridges, the rifle will probably feed them. That's why they're often chambered for .22 LR, Longs, or Shorts.

Lever-actions: Just about anyone who ever watched a Western can identify this all-American design, which is in no immediate danger of fading away despite its 19th century birth. Admittedly, there is a certain romantic aura associated with a classic levergun, and tradition plays a strong role. There are still plenty of centerfire versions roaming the deer woods where I live and, romance aside, they continue to fill freezers. For such hunters, a rimfire twin is a logical choice for use on smaller game or cans. Most will have tubular magazines and external hammers. A lever powers the bolt, feeds new cartridges, and re-cocks the rifle for subsequent shots. Like pumps, lever-actions are often designed to shoot the full spectrum of conventional .22-ammunition. Some are also sold in more potent rimfire calibers like the .22 Magnum.

Single-shots (bolt, break and falling-block actions): By far the simplest design is a single shot. Since a cartridge is manually inserted, load status can be easily verified. It's no coincidence that beginner rifles employ single-shot systems. Many are built as bolt-actions, but break barrel designs are also fairly common. Typically, the barrel will pivot downward on a hinge in the receiver, which exposes its chamber. These guns often have an external hammer that must be manually cocked prior to firing. Some are sold as multi caliber sets with extra centerfire and shotgun barrels. Less common are falling blocks that use a lever to elevate a breechblock mecha-

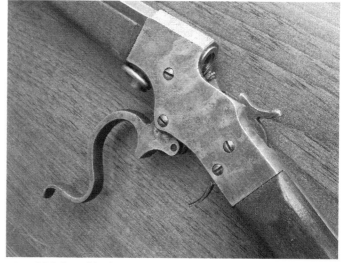

An old falling-block Stevens chambered for obsolete .32 rimfire cartridges.

nism. Most single-shot rifles are fairly inexpensive, simple, and tend to be lightweight. These traits offer appeal to younger shooters, but I'm not too wild about hammers and kids – at least, not without very close hands-on supervision. For beginners, a simple bolt-action is hard to beat. Most other repeating types can be manually loaded as single shots, but the process may prove difficult. It really boils down to individual rifle designs and ejection port clearance.

Oddballs: Two types that come to mind are those based on revolver-type actions and two-barrel combination guns. The latter operates as a break barrel, offering the option of a rifle or shotgun in one package. Either is relatively simple to operate, but both are really niche firearms.

WHICH ONE?

Good question! There are many different models and makes within each rifle type listed above. For example, when Ruger and twenty-two appear in the same sentence, many of us will think of their famous 10/22 semi-automatic - an all-time favorite plinker. Ruger also produces a very nice line of bolt-action rimfires. For someone considering their centerfire models, a small-bore Ruger "American" or pricier Model 77/22 companion piece will serve as a great small game hunting AND training rifle, capable of killing cans just as effectively as any centerfire.

Remington and Henry sell pumps. For the lever-action fans, Browning sells an interesting line, as do Marlin, Mossberg and Henry. These rifles also support ambidextrous use, which can come in handy if multiple users are envisioned. AR-15 shooters now have rimfire alternatives.

Most of these rifles are "repeaters". In other words, they offer the capability for fast follow-up shots. We'll take a closer look at each system, but a few other considerations remain…

"Clips", magazines & repeaters: Recently, during an AR-15 rifle school, we encountered some confusion among participants about magazine nomenclature. This was based on an old rimfire term frequently used to describe the feeding process of repeaters – a clip.

Repeating rifles will normally be fed by a either a detachable magazine or some sort of tubular arrangement. Once filled with cartridges, they both allow quick follow-up shots. The term "clip" is often applied to a detachable rimfire magazine. Technically, it isn't one, but the description has stuck. A good example of a true "clip" is the sheet metal eight-round cartridge holder used to reload the semi-automatic .30/06 M-1

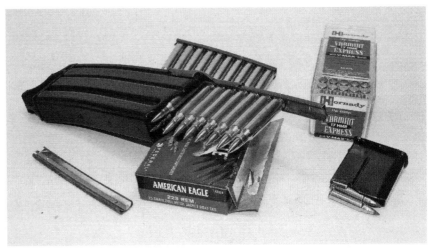

M-16 stripper "clip" system, and a .17 Hornady Magnum Rimfire detachable magazine.

Garand rifle of World War II fame. Stripper clips are another military design. They capture a stack of cartridges vertically by their rims, for fast manual loading via one quick shove with a thumb.

A true magazine is an actual component of a firearm. A detachable version is normally a metal (or polymer) box. It permits quick and convenient reloads if spares are on hand. The M16 rifle is a good example. Most Vietnam era magazines held 20 cartridges, and 30-round versions are now more common (in fact, either GI type can be quickly refilled using pre-loaded stripper clips).

Detachable-magazine rimfire rifles work similarly and, depending on the firearm, their capacity can run from as few as 5 rounds up to 25 or more. I generally prefer this system, but lost magazines are a concern. It's worth stocking up on a few spares, which are usually affordable. They are inserted vertically from un-

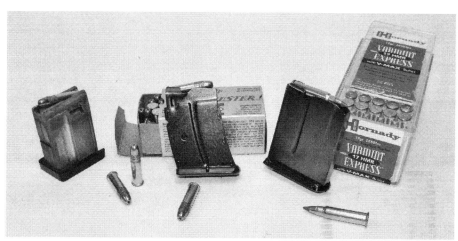

An assortment of detachable rimfire magazines.

derneath the action and, although most employ a fairly positive latch, it is possible for gravity to take over if carelessness kicks in. Others just become misplaced during routine storage. A great deal on a used rifle may not be so hot in the long haul without access to replacements. No stripper clip rimfire systems exist, but somehow the "clip" moniker has stuck.

Tubular magazines are normally an integral part of a rifle. Most hang underneath the barrel, and are loaded from the muzzle end. A few others are housed within the stock and loaded through the butt. Either design feeds horizontally by spring pressure exerted on a "follower", through a separate removable inner sleeve. Capacity is typically generous, providing 10 to 25 shots depending on the model and type of ammo used. However, reloading a tubular magazine is a slower process because cartridges are usually inserted individually. Unloading requires removal of the inner sleeve for dumping of live rounds. Care needs to be taken to keep extremities clear of the muzzle with barrel-mounted

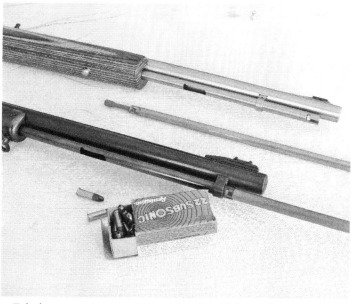

Tubular magazine assemblies, showing their loading ports and inner followers.

designs. Also, many tubular designs require an extra careful action check to ensure complete unloading. Although a high-visibility orange follower is common, the small and enclosed receiver can make it hard to see.

Sighting systems: The full gamut of available options will be covered later. The thing to remember for the time being is that the best rifles available can't perform without a suitable means to aim them.

Many .22 caliber rifles are equipped with iron sights. These are often of a rudimentary design consisting of a metal bead up front and an adjustable rear notch. Alignment on a target can provide hits at fairly close distances, but while they provide a reassuring backup system, some sort of optical aiming device affords better precision and increased range. Whatever device is chosen will need to be solidly coupled to the rifle, so mounting options will need consideration.

The tubular magazine on this Marlin shows an orange follower when empty. It still can be hard to see, especially in low light, so check it carefully!

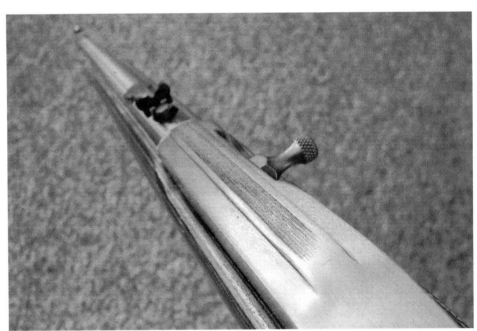

Iron sights and a grooved receiver for mounting of standard tip-off scope rings.

The most common rimfire systems employ parallel receiver grooves, spaced 3/8" apart. Corresponding scope rings are often referred to as "tip-offs", which clamp securely to the grooves. The European grooves are spaced a bit wider at 11mm. Ruger's Model 77 bolt-actions are machined for their rugged but proprietary clamping ring system. Their lower-priced "American" .22 rifle offers multiple mounting options, including dovetail grooves and the very popular Weaver bases. S&W's AR-22 has an integral Picatinny rail, which is dimensionally identical to an AR-15 "flat-top" receiver. This system is similar to the Weaver design, but standardized to military specifications (although there are subtle differences).

A Picatinny-type mounting system with Weaver-type scope rings.

Some oddball or older twenty-two rifles were designed for iron sights and lack the means to mount any optics. In other words, the best time to look for the features you'll need is *prior* to your purchase!

Intended use: Your anticipated needs should guide the final selection. A bush pilot might only want a barebones, lightweight rifle for emergency foraging in remote areas. Targets could include snowshoe hares, ptarmigan, or grouse, which are normally shot at fairly close range. For such use, any basic .22 would suffice. It would constitute just one part of a survival kit, along with spare ammo, flares, matches, a knife, compass, first aid supplies, communication device, and other gear.

Others may envision several uses. In the context of this book, survival will be foremost, the key elements being defense and subsistence. However, other uses *should* be considered:

Defense: None of the rimfire calibers are a great choice, due to their marginal punch. Among them, the .22 Magnum is your best bet, especially in a rifle barrel, which develops maximum velocity from this cartridge. Still, any firearm is better than none, and a barrage of .22 Long Rifle hollow-points could be a serious deterrent.

Subsistence: Use may involve survival forays, but in calmer times, it might also include legal small game hunts. Anything goes in a life-or-death situation, and a small caliber rifle will preserve edible meat. Try eating a small red squirrel or blackbird that's been shot with a high-power rifle. The head is a tiny target and a body shot will blow your dinner to smithereens. Species as large as deer could be taken at close range with a careful head shot from a .22 LR. It's neither recommended nor legal in most places, but it sure beats starving. A .22 is also fairly quiet with the right ammo. Meanwhile, the same rifle can help hone hunting skills on legal quarry, such as gray squirrels. It's a pastime, much like miniature big game hunting, and it is also entertaining!

The results of a well-spent morning in the woods with a .22 rifle.

Plinking: Targets could be cans on a log, fired shotgun shells, fruit, or commercial metal spinners. They are really up to the imagination of the shooter. The idea is to go out and have a good time. Add some safety-minded friends and competitive rivalry to improve everyone's shooting ability. It's probably safe to say that the majority of .22 rimfire ammunition is consumed during this pastime.

Training: In this case, the rimfire rifle will serve to improve skills with other, larger caliber firearms. If it is of similar design, overall proficiency will improve thanks to common operation. Any new or junior shooters are also best started on a small-scale rimfire, which produces less recoil and noise.

SUMMARY

For pure defensive use, consider something larger. A shotgun will do nicely, justifying its first gun safe slot. But with careful shopping, we can fill the other roles using just one rimfire rifle. This is a good thing, since there's more involved with firearms ownership than just a gun…

System (or overall) cost: Besides a rifle, we'll need a few accessories. A scope will top the list for many, and a bipod may make the list. Both have substantial cost, whereas other essentials like gun cases, spare magazines, and cleaning gear are relatively inexpensive. Since they all add up, we'll need budget wiggle room to acquire the pieces. These key components constitute our actual "system cost".

Ammunition plays an equally important part in the equation. A full understanding of available loads will not only fully exploit the system, but also guide us towards the right rifle.

CHAPTER 3

RIMFIRE AMMUNITION BASICS

The *Survival Guns* edition contains a Chapter titled "A Tutorial on Ammunition". An explanation of subjects such as cartridge design, nomenclature, calibers, and bullet weight is included. For the uninitiated, it provides a handy starting point for much of the following terminology. A graphic from that publication is included here:

The "rimfire" moniker refers to the ignition system of our oldest American cartridge design. The ancient .22 Short appeared in 1857 and has been in continuous production ever since. Today, it is just one of a whole series of very interesting offspring. A few larger-bore offerings appeared but such ammunition was obsolete before World War II. Smaller-bore cartridges have also come and gone, but the ones we'll examine here are, for the most part, still going. Below is a current list, assembled in order of power:

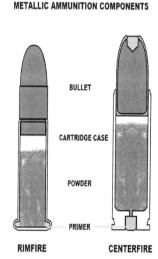

METALLIC AMMUNITION COMPONENTS

BULLET

CARTRIDGE CASE

POWDER

PRIMER

RIMFIRE   CENTERFIRE

Rimfire and centerfire cartridge designs.

Assembled and disassembled .22 LR cartridges. Note the firing pin indent on the fired case.

Rimfire calibers	Availability	Use
.22 Rimfire (in Short, Long & Long Rifle)	Most popular	*Mild report and low cost make .22 LR the top choice for plinking, target-shooting, pest-control and small game hunting inside 100 yards. Fires .223 caliber, 40 grain bullets up to 1400 fps. Several light-bullet versions in .22 Short, Long & Long Rifle provide other power levels for specialty uses.*
.22 Winchester Rimfire Magnum (.22 WMR)	Popular	*Provides a major power increase, driving .224 caliber, 40 grain bullets to over 1900 fps. Range increases by 50 yards and the power will handle larger varmints and fur-bearing animals. Expense and noise preclude plinking, but fall well below centerfire constraints.*
5mm Remington Magnum Rimfire	Near-obsolete	*A .20 caliber bottleneck cartridge similar in power to the .22 WMR. Fires a 38 grain bullet 2100 fps, but no new guns and scarce ammo render it a poor choice.*
.17 Hornady Mach 2 (.17 HM-2)	Waning	*Introduced 2004. Based on a necked down .22 LR case, it drives a very light 17 grain, .172 caliber bullet to 2100 fps. Noise is on par with .22 LR. Cost is greater, but so is range. Trajectory is similar to .22 WMR, but punch is less. Anticipated popularity was never achieved and sales have dropped.*
.17 Hornady Magnum Rimfire (.17 HRM)	Very popular	*Introduced 2002. Based on a necked down .22 WMR case, achieving over 2500 fps with a 17 grain bullet. Noise and cost are similar to .22 WMR, but trajectory is flatter, permitting hits on small varmints out to 150 yards. The .17 HMR is a huge hit, although wind affects the light bullets.*
.17 Winchester Super-Magnum	New in 2013	*The hottest performer, it's based on a necked down, .27 caliber ram-set cartridge. Drives a 25 grain .172 bullet to 3,000 fps for 200+ yard performance on small varmints. Cost is only slightly higher than .17 HMR ammo, but cartridges are larger, requiring purpose-built actions. Stay tuned…*

Not shown above are larger and now obsolete cartridges like .25 and .32 rimfires. Others still exist, including the Mexican-produced .17 Aguila, an ill-timed arrival coinciding with two domestically produced announcements. It is based on a necked down .22 Long Rifle. Some people claim it can be fired in a Hornady Mach 2 chamber, but I'll pass on that. The necks are different. Both appeared in 2002. The latter eclipsed the former, but ironically, the HM-2 is now losing ground. Such has been the case for a number of other cartridges, like the now obscure .22 Extra Long and .22 Automatic.

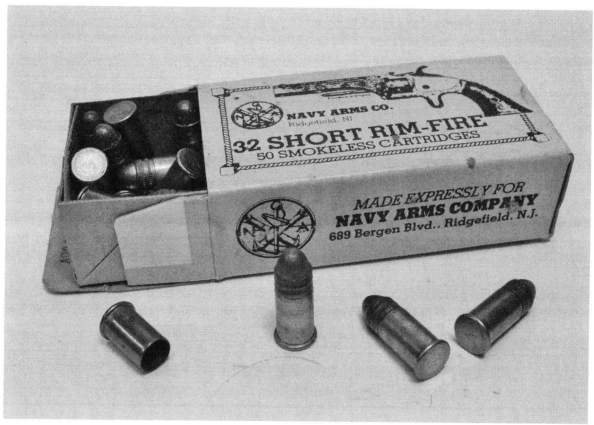

The now obsolete .32 Rimfire.

CONVENTIONAL .22 RIMFIRE AMMUNITION

Cartridges in this classification include .22 caliber BB Caps, CB Caps, Shorts, Longs, and Long Rifle denominations. Overall lengths and power vary, but they all share the same rim and case diameter. Each version, beginning with the stumpy little BB Cap, should fit in the longest one's chamber – cut for the aptly named Long Rifle cartridge. Expanding on the .22 Rimfire classification listed above, we'll begin at the bottom of the power totem pole and progress through the options.

.22 BB Cap: This old load is actually the true originator of all rimfire loads in use today. While the .22 Short is the oldest American rimfire and our first metallic cartridge, the European .22 Bullet Breech Cap predates it by at least 10 years. It is very low-powered and expels a .22 caliber lead ball or small conical projectile by the force of the priming mix alone. It was used in Flobert parlor rifles, one of which I discovered in my grandfather's ancient golf club bag. The single-shot Belgian-made rifle and cartridge became popular as an indoor parlor or shooting gallery combination, but use waned as improved iterations appeared. Today, BB Caps are a scarce commodity, although it may be possible to locate some. The label will probably say RWS. You can fire BB Caps in a standard .22 LR chamber, but the rounds will probably need to be manually inserted. Power and dimensions will prevent proper function in most repeating designs, an exception being revolvers. In a rifle, the report is nearly absent and often not as loud as the fall of a firing pin. The BB Cap's anemic power makes it a poor choice for critter control and raises the risks of ricochets. In certain cases, it might be possible to lodge the bullet in a bore.

.22 CB Cap: Power-wise, the present day CB Cap probably approximates the power of the original .22 Short. The cartridge case and bullet are the same, but nowadays, a CB Cap contains a smaller powder charge. The result is slower velocity and a less noisy shot. Muzzle velocity will run around 750 fps with its 29 grain bullet, and the report will be quieter than many airguns. A similar and more recent CB Cap version is a mild .22 Long, which improves feeding in .22 LR actions. However, due to the greater case volume and random distribution of its powder charge, the longer-cased CB load may be somewhat less accurate. The only reliable way to tell involves careful testing of each in the intended rifle. Typical .22 LR accuracy-testing protocol involves firing five 5-shot groups off a good sandbag rest at 50 yards. With CB Caps and Shorts, I cut that distance in half. In other words, either load is a close-range proposition. Still, I find them to be very useful little cartridges.

In many rifles, you can clearly hear the firing pin strike the case rim of a CB Cap. The report is just a quiet snap, and the sound of the bullet hitting some objects will be louder than the shot. A simple, longer-barreled bolt-action is just the ticket for this effect. My old Remington single-shot Model 510 is the go-to CB and Short rifle. Either round can just be tossed into the solid-bottom receiver so the bolt can shove it home. The small powder charge is consumed inside its 24-inch barrel, making for an ultra-quiet report. In other actions with small ejection ports, loading can be a royal pain. The little cartridges are tough to handle for those with bigger fingers. It's generally doable, but you have to hold your mouth just right.

On the other hand, those .22 rifles designed to run with Shorts will usually cycle CB Caps. Marlin's Model 39A lever-action holds more than half a box: 26 rounds! Again, its 24-inch barrel is extremely quiet. The Remington pump I owned fed CB Caps like a champ and shot them more accurately than any other rifle I've tried. The reason remains a mystery.

The only semi-auto I'm aware of that will properly digest CB Caps is Ruger's 10/22 with specially produced Volquartsen parts. VQ sells a CB Cap kit consisting of a lightweight aluminum bolt, low-powered spring, and modified magazine. It sounds like a fun conversion, but would take time to install. The more practical alternative would be to use a standard Ruger and CB Longs, manually cycling the bolt.

In a handgun, CB Caps are a whole lot louder, although far from deafening. The same feeding issues occur with semi-autos, but a revolver won't know the difference. The report will be a bit louder, owing to the barrel/cylinder gap – a small price to pay for positive function. Let's put it this way; you could probably get away with shooting CB Caps in a rifle. You probably couldn't with a handgun, at least, not in a settled area. Also, just because they seem wimpy doesn't mean a CB Cap is safe to shoot without concerns for a proper backstop. Carrying distance will be greatly reduced, but lethality still exists. I've also noticed an increased propensity for ricochets. I set my pump CB Cap rifle up to practice thrown targets, but quit shooting after hearing lots of whining bullets. It was pretty unnerving.

Don't be surprised if the low-velocity bullets impact differently. You'll likely need a new zero due to decreased velocity. Also, a ring of fouling and lead will accumulate in a .22 Long Rifle chamber, just ahead of the shorter round. The eventual result will be difficult chambering and possible extraction failures. This is a safety concern if live rounds become lodged in a chamber. The extractor jaws will probably slip over the cartridge rim. It's easy to miss this and can advance to prying with knives or other instruments, all capable of detonating the priming compound. The fix: brush out the chamber (or chambers) periodically. Better yet, try CCI CB Longs. Their cases are the same length as Long Rifles.

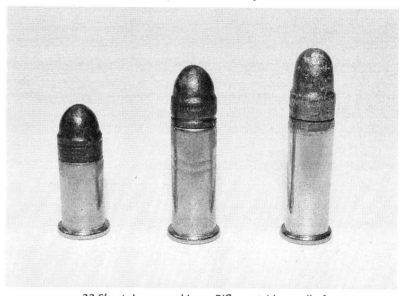

.22 Short, Long, and Long Rifle cartridges, all of which will fire in a LR chamber.

The CB Cap is a useful stealth-mode load, capable of killing small game like squirrels at reasonable distances. For some folks, it will render an airgun unnecessary. The report may actually be quieter, and the 29 grain bullet with its 700 fps muzzle velocity will hit harder than most "Magnum" air rifles.

.22 Short: This venerable circa 1857 load only accounts for a small portion of overall rimfire production, but it's still going today. Ammo will be a bit harder to find and prices will probably be higher, due to the sheer volume of .22 Long Rifle output. The stiffer .22 Short high-velocity loads propel a 29 grain bullet to almost 1100 fps. The more sedate standard-velocity loads are about 100 fps faster than CB Caps, clocking around 830 fps. Both are lots of fun to shoot and offer interesting pest control opportunities. Unless a repeating firearm is specifically designed to operate with Shorts, it probably won't feed them. Today, a niche market exists in high-end Olympic class target pistols, which are designed for small-bore rapid-fire events. Shorts aren't for everyone but, analogous to the target-shooting niche, they do occupy a specialty role when low noise or limited range are concerns.

.22 Long: The next evolution in power arrived in 1871 by lengthening the Short's cartridge case to hold more powder. The result was a velocity increase of roughly another 100 fps. The power race was on, and within nine years the Long had been eclipsed. As a result, it's an obsolete load from the standpoint of firearms production. However, enough old guns exist to warrant continued production of .22 Long ammunition, with much of that geared towards the previously mentioned CB Long. You can fire .22 Long cartridges in a .22 LR chamber, but the ammo probably won't function correctly in semi-automatic firearms. Since cost won't be less than Shorts nor performance better than Long Rifle ammo, the .22 Long isn't worth the bother.

.22 Long Rifle: The design dates back to 1887 and has become hugely popular today. If you go to a sporting goods retailer and ask for a brick of twenty-twos, odds are high that the clerk will hand you a box labeled .22 LR. The Long Rifle combines the Long's case length with a heavier 40 grain bullet, developing a muzzle velocity of around 1100 fps in standard form. The high-velocity loads are listed at around 1250 fps, but the Long Rifle has been tinkered with to the point where the lines begin to blur. So many different .22 LR loads have been produced that we can break them into sub-categories for a closer look:

Standard velocity loads: Most target ammunition falls into this category. When the object is to punch a hole in paper, a well-built lead bullet will do the job. The best loads from companies like Eley or Lapua are carefully assembled to Olympic match grade standards, and are priced accordingly. More pedestrian versions like Winchester's T-22 offer a casual target shooting alternative. Some firearms, particularly a few .22 target pistols, are designed for standard-velocity ammunition. On the other hand, a good many semi-automatic sporting rifles are built to digest high speeds. Function with milder standard loads may suffer as a result. Without guidance from a manufacturer, some experimentation may be necessary.

High speeds: A large portion of .22 Long Rifle ammunition meets this loose classification. Often, the bullets will have copper-washed surfaces and hollow-point tips. The cavity increases expansion and shaves a couple grains in weight, which increases velocity. The market is geared towards plinking, informal target shooting, and hunting. Smaller edible game like gray squirrels may be a bit banged up, but anchoring power will be improved over plain round-nose bullets.

Hypervelocity loads: CCI's "Stinger" really changed the game, combining a slightly lengthened case with a light 32 grain hollow-point bullet. Velocity increased to over 1600 fps, spawning a new generation of hypervelocity loads. The light, fast bullets have flatter trajectories, but are fairly destructive on edible game. Accuracy varies and may be perfectly useable, although not match grade. The Stinger's longer case can cause problems in some match chambers, which are close-tolerance for improved accuracy. The Bentz chamber is one design you'll often see in precision 10/22 barrels. Tolerances are tighter than a standard chamber, but dimensions are optimized for semi-automatic feeding. The longer Stinger case can impact the tight forward chamber edge, and may damage that area. Extraction of *any* live rounds in Bentz chambers is frequently a problem, since the bullet is a tight fit. Among other issues is the concern raised by non-extracted live rounds.

Subsonic loads: On the other end of the spectrum, slower loads are becoming popular. Supersonic bullets produce a fairly sharp crack, so holding velocity below that speed makes an audible difference in noise. Most .22 subsonic offerings run around 1050, but CCI sells a "Quiet" load rated at 710 fps. Power will be insufficient to run most semi-automatics. Aguila has gone to the extreme with their Super-Sniper Subsonic load that fires a very heavy 60 grain bullet at just below 1000 fps. It's an interesting way to combine extra punch with subsonic velocity for effective suppressed (or silenced) performance. However, heavier bullets generally require faster rifling twists. The common .22 twist of one complete revolution in 16 inches (1x16), will likely result in poor accuracy. The fix involves a faster rate like 1x9, but changing barrels can involve major surgery. Thankfully, Ruger's barrel attachment system permits hobby-gunsmith replacement with quicker-twist tubes.

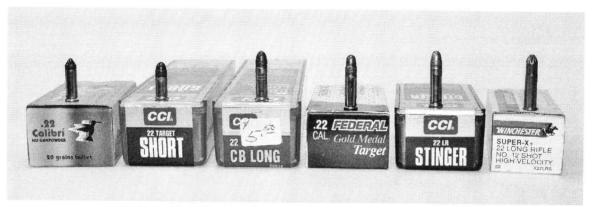

Various .22 rimfire cartridges capable of firing in a .22 LR chamber.

Other .22 pipsqueak loads: A few offerings I'd lump into this category are Aguila's Calibri and Super Calibri, which expel a very light 20 grain bullet to 375 and 500 fps, respectively. I'd worry about shooting them in a rifle. You'd run the risk of a stuck bullet due to bore friction. In fact, it would be entirely possible to stick several – something I've seen with squib .38 bullets. They'd be just about impossible to dislodge, and the barrel would probably be ringed. Some folks get away with them, but some do not. A revolver would be the better choice, but caution is still advised. Report in a rifle is just about nonexistent. Handguns will be louder, approximating a ramset report. When all is said and done, CB Caps may be the better choice.

Shot loads: Another oddball variation, which has been around for years, fires very small birdshot pellets. Rifles have been produced with smoothbore barrels specifically for these shells. Obviously, the capacity of a tiny .22 LR case will greatly limit the amount of shot. To maintain some semblance of pattern density, #12 pellets are commonly employed. Their tiny mass really limits terminal performance, but so-called "rat-shot" does have some uses. I've used it for indoor rodent extermination where distances were short and the targets were furtive. Some folks prefer .22 shot-shells for use in revolvers against snakes, where ranges are measured in feet. A 10-yard shot with these loads would be more miraculous than a 70-yard shot with a conventional shotgun. Think close – very close – range.

I once discovered mice in the basement and decided to liven up an otherwise dull winter by going on safari. First, I decided to shoot some patterns. Using mouse silhouettes drawn on cardboard boxes, I let fly from several different rifles. One useful discovery was that my old Marlin Model 39 Mountie shot noticeably better patterns. It's just theory, but the improvement may be attributable to its Micro-Groove rifling, which is much finer than conventional types. Range could be extended by two whopping yards, out to around 7 paces. I donned safety glasses, procured a flashlight and carefully waited for shots that wouldn't jeopardize the freezer or water heater. Yes, I am easily entertained.

OTHER .22 RIMFIRE CARTRIDGES

The .22 loads we've covered so far have a few things in common. First, they use a heeled bullet (with the exception of shot-loads) which is sometimes referred to as "outside lubricated". The actual bullet is the same diameter as its case, and a smaller-diameter shank protrudes inside to accept a crimp. The external portion of the bullet is copper-plated or lubricated for feeding and barrel cleanliness. Bore diameter will be about .223 caliber.

Examining a .22 Magnum, you'll notice critical differences. Besides being much longer, the case diameter will be slightly fatter. The bullet's diameter will be constant and smaller than its case. It will probably be jacketed (or plated), and sized for a .224 caliber bore. These dimensional changes ensure that a higher-pressure .22 WMR won't fit in a .22 Long Rifle chamber. A .22 Long Rifle cartridge could be inserted in a .22 Magnum chamber, but firing it would be very unwise. The smaller case will probably rupture, venting hot gases and debris back towards the shooter. In other words, you can't safely shoot .22 LR in a .22 WMR chamber. Some manufacturers like Ruger solved this problem by offering revolvers with two different cylinders. Accuracy may be less than stellar with .22 LR loads (but still acceptable), due to the necessarily larger .224 bore.

.22 Winchester Rim Fire (.22 WRF): I got a lesson in pressure at an early age after buying an old Winchester Model 1890 pump from a high school crony. The barrel was stamped .22 WRF, which, to me, meant twenty-two something. I dropped in a .22 Long Rifle and experienced an exciting reaction which indicated all was not well. Not being the brightest bulb in the circuit, I still managed to exercise what small amount of deductive powers remained, and ceased fire. The .22 WRF was introduced for Winchester's Model 1890 and provided another rung up the ladder in rimfire power. Velocity was around 1450 fps with a flat-nosed .224 diameter, 454 grain bullet. Like the .22 Magnum, its bullet slips inside the cartridge case. The lead bullet's lubricating grooves are beneath the case mouth, hence the "inside lubricated" term.

.22 Winchester Magnum Rimfire (.22 WMR): The .22 Magnum represents a quantum leap in rimfire performance. In 1959, Winchester souped up the old .22 WRF, stretching its length and reinforcing the case to withstand much higher pressures. The resulting .22 Magnum broke entirely new ground, launching a 40 grain bullet to nearly 2000 fps from a rifle barrel. I knew one of its designers, who shared much interesting information about the developmental process. Since then, the .22 Magnum has had more than half a century to mature. Ammunition is now widely available in several bullet weights and designs. It's actually a very useful cartridge with considerably more thump than any .22 LR load. The .22 WMR produces a noticeably louder report, but is still well below the signature of most centerfire rifle cartridges.

30 grain loads: These light bullets boost muzzle velocity to 2200 fps, which flattens trajectory slightly while producing destructive wounds on small varmints such as prairie dogs. It's a great varmint pick, but not the right choice for small game hunting.

40 grain loads: For larger animals such as foxes, the heavier and tougher bullets would be better choices. Loads are available in two different designs. The more popular hollow-points will cover

most chores, although expansion will tear up small game. Winchester sells a 40 grain full-metal jacket with a small flat tip. It was designed for small game hunters and trappers and, since it doesn't expand, meat or pelt damage will be minimal. Velocity is rated identically at 1910 fps. Theoretically, you could shoot either type with one common zero. Unfortunately, things don't always work out that way in real life. You won't know for sure until you shoot each load on paper.

45 grain load: Winchester's Dynapoint bullet is slower than the lighter bullets, but has a bit more mass. It's actually similar to the old .22 WRF load, making it a good choice for use on small game. Velocity listed at 1550 fps and the bullet is a plated hollow-point. The best news is the price of under $10 per 50-round box. Hornady has a new FTX "Critical Defense" load, designed for handguns. It is listed at around 1000 fps, but in a rifle, velocity improves to 1700 fps, producing, in Hornady's words, "devastating terminal performance".

The .22 Winchester Magnum Rimfire (.22 WMR).

50 grain load: Federal sells the heaviest .22 WMR: a 50 grain hollow-point with a rated muzzle velocity of 1530 fps. It supposedly produces somewhat less meat damage than a 40 grain HP, while increasing penetration. Out of all .22 WMR offerings, this would be my choice for coyotes. As an eastern woods load, its trajectory would be less of a concern.

Shot loads: CCI sells a .22 WMR cartridge with a plastic capsule "bullet" that contains a tiny load of #11 shot. For a brief while, Marlin sold a smoothbore variation of their .22 WMR bolt-action called the Garden Gun. Supposedly, patterns and range were greatly improved with hope of dispatching small pest birds like starlings out to around 15 yards. From rifled barrels, the same load may offer slight improvement over .22 LR shot, but range will likely be cut by half, down to around 6-7 yards.

I know a well-respected Maine hunter who has shot a pile of very large eastern coyotes with his .22 Magnum. This was surprising news, but he did say they were shot in thick woods at fairly close range. Most folks will opt for a more potent cartridge like a .223. Amazingly, in Maine, the .22 Magnum is legal for deer. No doubt, a number of them have been shot with it, too. I wouldn't be surprised if even more have been killed by .22 Long Rifles, from careful head shots administered by poachers. Does that justify either load as a recommended choice? Heck no! Get a bigger gun.

Again, you cannot shoot .22 Long Rifle in a .22 Magnum! Also, cost of the latter is much greater, ruling it out as a high-volume plinker. Still, pricing is substantially below centerfire costs. A box of 50 .22 WMR is also cheaper than a box of centerfire pistol cartridges. We'll look at the .22 Magnum again in the handgun book. For now, don't expect performance to come anywhere close to what can be achieved with a rifle.

Summing things up, in a rifle, the .22 WMR will perform at 100 yards, just a touch better than a .22 LR will at the muzzle. In a revolver, the .22 WMR will produce muzzle velocities roughly the equivalent of a .22 LR when fired from a rifle. You might as well plan on losing somewhere around 500 fps in your handgun.

The .22 Magnum is a fairly accurate cartridge. I've shot plenty of 1.25-inch 5-shot groups at 100 yards from a number of different rifles, including an H&K Model 300 semi-automatic. As mentioned before, I've shot one-inch groups at 100 yards from two different Ruger Model 77/22 rifles. Owing to its velocity, the .22 WMR also shoots quite a bit flatter than a .22 LR. Using the latest hot-shot loads like Hornady's 30 grain V-Max, which has a very aerodynamic plastic-tipped bullet, zeroed at 100 yards, groups will strike within ½ inch of the crosshairs, out to 125 yards. Even with more conventional 40 grain loads, range can be extended at least 50 yards beyond a .22 LR.

The .22 Magnum is a great choice, especially for those who don't hand-load. I really like it in repeating rifles. Since it is non-reloadable, empty cases can be shucked without concerns over retrieval. Although it really isn't a plinking round, cost is still fairly reasonable.

Lastly, the old .22 WRF cartridge can be fired in most .22 WMR chambers. You can think of it as a .22 Magnum "Short". CCI doesn't recommend the practice in revolvers, owing to their heavy jacketed bullet. Supposedly, the barrel/cylinder gap can bleed off enough pressure to lower velocity and lodge a bullet. The .22 WRF Winchester should safely fire in most other .22 Magnums, but might not properly feed in some repeaters due to shorter overall length. I mention this just in case the planet is reduced to smoking rubble and you happen upon an old, funny-looking box labeled ".22 Winchester Rimfire". In fact, modern production runs appear now and then in deference to the older rifles. For further confusion, the old and obsolete .22 Remington Special is essentially the same cartridge.

SMALL-BORE RIMFIRES

"Small-bore" is a relative term. The .22s are by no means large. But one thing you can always depend on is ballistic evolution. The original rimfire cartridges have been necked down and tweaked, resulting in some intriguing variations.

5mm Remington Magnum Rimfire: This little cartridge illustrates why, from a survival point of view, it isn't wise to embrace every new technology. The .20 caliber round was Remington's answer to Winchester's popular .22 Magnum. It had a unique, necked cartridge, which fired a 38 grain bullet at 2100 fps, making it the rimfire speed king when it appeared in 1970. The shooting public yawned, and the 5mm Remington had slipped into obsolescence within 5 years. Those shooters who scurried out and bought a Remington bolt-action Model 591 or 592 (clip or tube-fed) were soon left without ammo. Thompson Center also chambered some Contender single-shot pistol barrels for the 5mm RMR.

Maybe it was an idea ahead of its time. The recent .17 HMR caught on like wildfire. Regardless, today, finding 5mm ammo is a challenge. The well went completely dry for a long time, but recently Centurion/Aguila has introduced a faster 30 grain load that hits 2300 fps. If things go completely bust, good luck finding some at a local hardware store.

.17 Hornady Mach 2: Hornady jumped on the initial .17 rimfire craze and, in 2004, they necked the .22 Long Rifle "Stinger" case down to .17 caliber. The result was a miniaturized version of the larger .22 WMR-based .17 HMR, which would fit into .22 LR actions. The new HM-2 gave up 500 fps, compared to its bigger .17 HMR brother, but still achieved 2100 fps with the same flyweight 17 grain bullets.

Various rifle manufacturers tooled up for the cartridge, and it wasn't long before .17 HM-2 conversion kits appeared for Ruger's 10/22 rifles. The zippy cartridge needed a heavier bolt to delay unlocking of the blowback system. Achieving the proper balance was difficult, as many people soon found out.

The hotter and pre-existing .17 HRM may have already stolen the limelight, although the Mach 2 seemed like a good idea at the time. I considered a .17 HM-2 for use on crows, the idea being that the very light bullet would be safer to fire at targets in trees. In the end, I just stuck with a .17 HMR that was already on hand. That mindset may explain the ebbing tide of the smaller round. If you already have a .17 Mach 2, you have a very interesting little cartridge. In the same size actions, it shoots flatter than a .22 LR, extending range to at least 100 yards without additional noise. Trajectory will be more like a .22 Magnum, but with less than half the bullet weight, its punch will be diminished.

For the time being, .17 Mach 2 ammunition is available. Savage still lists bolt-action rifles. Recent trends may put it on the same track as the 5mm Remington Magnum Rimfire, but only time will tell.

.17 Hornady Magnum Rimfire (.17 HMR): After 150 years of metallic cartridge development, little is new under the sun. Nevertheless, once in a blue moon, a major milestone occurs. Happily, the .17 HMR fits this bill. It took off like a rocket in 2002, greatly exceeding anticipated sales. Necking the .22 Magnum's case to .17 caliber resulted in a sleek little bottle-necked cartridge capable of launching a miniature, 17 grain polymer-tipped bullet at around 2550 fps. Besides a flat trajectory, the icing on the cake was a remarkable level of accuracy. Of a few favorite cartridges, the .17 HMR is near the top of my list.

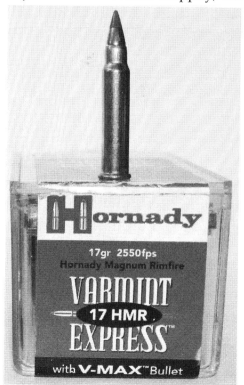

Shortly after its debut, I bought the Anschutz Model 1517 rifle. My old Leupold 4x12 VXII AO scope was pressed into service, and the fun began. I'll typically experiment with different ammo brands in search of the ultimate load, but this rifle caused an exception. On its maiden range trip, the first five-shot group, which I fired at 50 yards, went into about ¼ inch. Moving back to 100 yards, things opened up a bit – to ¾ inch. I was shooting Hornady 17 grain ammo and so far, have really never seen any reason to switch.

15.5 grain loads: CCI and Hornady also sell lead-free loads weighing 16 and 15.5 grains, respectively. The main market for these is areas where use of lead-core bullets is restricted. California ground squirrel hunters use them with success.

The amazing little .17 Hornady Magnum Rimfire.

17 grain loads: These are the most popular choice for good reason. The lighter loads aren't any faster and the heavier ones are significantly slower. The little polymer-tipped 17 grain bullets exploit the full potential of the .17 HMR in accuracy, range, and tissue destruction. It's a small caliber varmint hunter's dream in areas where noise and ricochet must be minimized.

20 grain loads: Slightly heavier 20 grain bullets are available for those inclined to experiment. Supposedly, they're more heavily constructed for use on small game. Velocity drops by nearly 200 fps, which probably helps limit expansion. The CCI FMJ may be just the ticket for small game hunters.

One thing to watch out for during accuracy testing is wind. It doesn't take much to drift the tiny bullets and negatively affect your groups. One morning, I lucked into dead calm air with perfect light. Shooting as carefully as possible off a good sandbag rest at 100 yards, I managed to record a stunning ¼ inch group. Admittedly, this one was probably a fluke. However, after seeing a number of sub-MOA groups from several different rifles, it's safe to conclude that the .17 HMR is plenty accurate.

The .17 HMR is useful because it really falls into a distinct niche, somewhere between a .22 LR and .223 Remington. This trait can be beneficial in settled areas where noise and range are issues. The report is on par with the .22 Magnum, but for soft targets like crows or other small varmints, effective range is greater due to the .17 HMR's flatter trajectory. I have a holdover and wind drift chart taped to the side of my Anschutz. After trying a few different zero distances, I settled on 100 yards. I just hold dead-on anything inside 130 yards. At 150 yards, I hold about 2 ½ inches high.

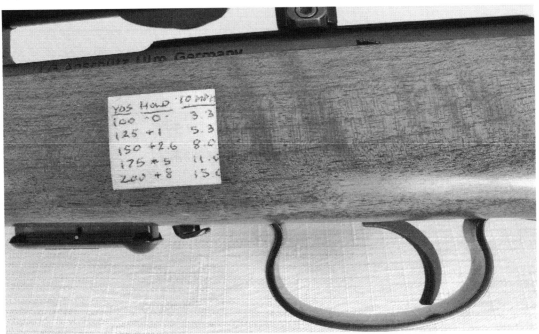

A handy reference for the .17 HMR. Note the 10 MPH wind data.

One time a friend and I set paintballs on golf tees and sniped them from various distances out to around 60 yards. He had a high-end Volquartsen 10/22 clone chambered for .22 Magnum, which was a real tack driver. I used my trusty .17 HMR Anschutz. Both were sufficiently accurate for the task at hand, but the advantage of the little .17's flat trajectory was clearly illustrated. I only needed to worry about maintaining the wobble of my crosshairs within the paintballs. My buddy had to deal with holdover as well. We both had 100-yard zeros, and at 50 yards the .17 bullets hit just a tenth of an inch higher. The .22 WMR was up almost an inch, which caused the air to turn blue for a while. On a target measuring 0.680", this was a problem. Thanks to multiple shooting opportunities, the correct holdover was soon deduced, but we don't always have that luxury afield.

Fortunately, most real-life targets will be quite a bit larger. Still, I've really come to depend on the ability of the .17 HMR to thread its bullets through tiny openings. A latticework of branches, which would normally be a real obstacle, can be surgically penetrated with a well-aimed shot. Many crows have plummeted from lofty perches after carefully woven bullets found their mark. As an eastern hunter, where ranges are seldom long, the little round has replaced the .223 for much of my varmint hunting. Besides the quieter report, the tiny bullet just seems a whole lot safer, especially when pruning crows from trees.

Things get more challenging in the vast expanse of the open west. Incessant wind and long distance pose real challenges for the tiny load. One morning back in 2004, the wind slacked on a South Dakota prairie dog shoot. The .17 HMR was still fairly new, so we dragged out our rifles and went to work and shot several hundred. Those inside 150 yards were hammered fairly hard but, at greater distances, effectiveness diminished on the guinea pig-sized gophers. My sidekick, Mike, was using a Burris Ballistic Plex scope with very useful holdover lines. Although it was clearly a stunt, I watched him

flip a sod poodle at 400 yards. Five years later in Nebraska's panhandle, we observed similar performance. Calm conditions were essential for mass destruction, which confined our shooting to small periods of just a few hours. Still, the .17 Hornady Rimfire Magnums were an absolute blast. Recoil was nonexistent, so hits or misses could be readily observed. Puffs of dust indicated the needed windage or holdover corrections. The mild report didn't shake up the prairie dogs too badly. Repeat shot opportunities helped rack up the body count. Barrel heating was never really a problem. With a rangefinder in hand, things were good.

Perfect .17 HMR quarry, a prairie dog nailed by his oversized doorway.

Mid-winter red fox with lots of thick fur, perhaps the practical upper limit for the .17 HMR.

Ten years of continuous use have provided some experience from which to draw conclusions. The .17 HMR is hell on crows, killing them like lightning. Squirrel-sized animals will be shellacked, but meat damage will be excessive. It works on woodchucks with upper body shots, out to around 150 yards. No doubt a number of coyotes have been killed with the .17 HMR. However, I wouldn't want to tackle anything larger than a fox. For larger furbearers, the .22 WMR would probably be a better choice. In other words, the .17 Hornady Magnum is really small-varmint round, albeit a very useful one in areas where range, ricochets, or noise are issues.

One thing you'll need is a good .17 caliber one-piece cleaning rod. A coated one might be a safer bet. The one I have works, but I'm careful not to apply too much force. It's not much thicker than a car antenna, and could pop into flex mode without any notice. The last thing I want is a ding in the barrel, so a pull-though flexible system is the safest bet.

.17 Winchester Super-Mag: Oh boy, here's a hot new number. In fact, it's so new that few people have shot it extensively. The box says "varmint & coyote", bearing a connotation of more power, which it does in fact have. Winchester modified a .27 caliber power-fastener cartridge capable of handling higher pressure. Their 20 grain bullet hits 3,000 fps and a heavier 25 grain load does 2,600 fps. The lighter load should permit dead-on holds out to 200 yards. The heavier bullet would be the coyote choice. With either, wind resistance will be much improved over the .17 HMR. Ammunition costs more, but is listed at only around $3.00 per box. Right now, market forces have pushed the real cost skyward. Assuming costs come down to their listed levels, the extra three bucks seems like a small additional price to pay considering the major leap forward in performance.

Savage came out with a brand new and affordable rifle, the "B-Mag", built just for the new .17 WSM. I've handled one and found it surprisingly lightweight. The action is a bit bigger than their standard rimfire design, and it cocks on closing. The new cartridge has a tougher case, and needs a harder firing pin strike for positive ignition. Savage says it's easier to cock a stiffer striker by pushing your hands together, which explains the new design.

Winchester chambered some of their elegant single-shot Model 1885 for the same load. I've been trying to resist this reincarnation of the John Browning-designed "low wall" for years. It's really too pretty for serious survival-type use, but makes for an intriguing combination.

It will be interesting to see what impact the new Winchester round has on Hornady's currently popular .17 HMR. Meanwhile, from a strictly pragmatic viewpoint, the lack of widespread ammunition makes the new .17 Super Mag a questionable choice.

RIMFIRE CARTRIDGES FOR SURVIVAL SITUATIONS

One could question the very idea of considering a rimfire during perilous circumstances. But let's not forget the AR-7 developed for Air Force crewmembers. Any gun is better than no gun, and sometimes, a quiet gun is desirable. Two principle uses during dire straits include defense and foraging. We examined these roles from a rifle perspective. Now, let's consider ammunition.

Defensive rimfire calibers: While just about all of the rimfire cartridges we've examined have hunting potential, none are really first-rate defensive choices. It's probably safe to say that cemeteries contain legions of hapless .22 Rimfire victims. It's also a fairly safe bet that many did not immediately succumb. You can kill a one ton steer with a properly placed .22 Long Rifle bullet. The operative phrase is "properly placed". A determined attacker needs to be stopped immediately. With adrenaline flowing, even in the best of a bad situation, a surgical shot is unlikely. A whole bunch of shots would be better, but again, there are no guarantees. The .22 Magnum would be your best bet, owing to its higher velocity and tougher bullet which is still only 40 grains. Granted, a 50 grain load is also available. The additional weight comes with a cost, which in this case amounts to nearly 500 fps of velocity loss, or a 1500 fps muzzle velocity. I'd choose this load for defense, banking on its slightly tougher and heavier bullet to improve penetration. We're talking about rifles. Things change drastically in handgun barrels. The .22 WMR does have a small following with a corresponding market of small-frame revolvers.

Hunting rimfire calibers: All of the rimfire calibers have hunting merits if their limitations are recognized. When the principle objective involves putting food on the table, a good rifle chambered for the ubiquitous .22 may be the best bet. Plain Jane .22 LR rounds are available just about anywhere one could expect to find ammunition. With the right bullet, game up to the size of a raccoon can be taken with a well-placed .22 Long Rifle. For sure, much larger animals have fallen to this round, including deer poached on the sly after dark. But there's a difference between practical reality and a stunt. Don't hunt deer with this cartridge unless you'll otherwise starve. In that case, a head shot will be necessary.

Believe it or not, that's pretty much the same story with woodchucks. You can certainly kill a groundhog with a well-placed upper body shot, but odds are good that it will die in a burrow. They're tough animals! For anything in this league, hollow-point bullets should be chosen. The smaller but edible gray squirrel is also fairly tenacious. A high-velocity HP will kill them cleanly, but the expanding bullet will tear up much meat. The fix involves a load like CCI's SGB, which stands for "small game bullet", possessing a flat tip. Remington's subsonic HP is my favorite squirrel load because it is fairly quiet and not overly destructive. It provides a bit of leeway over solids, which really should be used for headshots. A gray squirrel is small enough as it is, so the upper body provides a slightly bigger target. For anyone shooting Shorts or CB Caps, head shots will be required. They'll then work fine at modest ranges, and are safer when shooting skyward. Incidentally, be sure to read the warning label printed on the box. A .22 LR can travel a mile, retaining enough energy to prove lethal. Anything that goes up WILL come down, and if you shot it, you own it.

Speer's GDHP stands for "Gold Dot Hollow-Point". The SB indicates "short-barrel". This load is geared specifically for defensive handgun use, but it'll work in a rifle.

One thing going for the plain-vanilla .22 is its ability to digest multiple flavors, ranging from CB Caps through hypersonics. If ammo is scarce and you can't find exactly what you want, an older, dust-covered box of .22 Shorts should work in a pinch.

I don't have any experience with the .17 Mach 2. Although its bullet is tiny, at 2000 fps I'd expect to lose some meat. The trouble is that ammunition could be difficult to locate. Anyone owning one should stock up on ammo.

The .17 Hornady Magnum will definitely cause some damage. It is primarily a varmint round, and a very useful one at that. On edible game, headshots will be necessary. You might want to go for the heavier, 20 grain bullet and zero accordingly.

The .22 Magnum, on the other hand, is an excellent woods round choice. Where legal, it is sometimes used to harvest wild turkeys. Unlike the .22 LR, the hotter .22 WMR will reliably anchor woodchucks within reasonable distances out to 100 yards or thereabouts. If you did accidentally stumble into a real-life scene from *Deliverance*, the .22 Magnum would be the rimfire you'd want. Its improved performance comes at a price beyond the actual increased cost. The .22 WMR will be louder, and could also be harder to find than conventional .22 LR ammo.

Killing power: Actual "killing power" can be tough to define. Many formulas have been created to quantify so-called stopping power, but to my mind, it's just not an exact science. We often hear conversations comparing the effectiveness of one caliber to another but, interestingly, just about no one considers bullet construction. An expanding or non-expanding bullet of the same weight, traveling at the same velocity, will have similar energy. Impact force is commonly expressed as "foot-pounds". A 40 grain .22 Magnum bullet delivers around 325 ft. lbs. at the muzzle – roughly 185 ft. lbs. more than the same weight bullet from the fastest .22 Long Rifle. Obviously, the .22 Magnum hits harder. However, the non-expanding solid version may actually cause less tissue destruction than a .22 LR hollow-point. For this reason, I've chosen to skip energy figures. For anyone interested, the information is readily available. Instead, I'm including this chart, which is presented strictly from personal experience. Comparisons are based on fairly common representations of available loads. The high velocity .22 Long Rifle shown is a 38 grain hollow-point. The .22 Magnum ratings are based on 40 grain HPs. I'm sure plenty of folks will disagree. Remember, this is just a generalized representation of my own experience based on plenty of deceased critters. Coyotes could have been listed, but I honestly don't have experience using any loads shown below. Since we have to draw the line somewhere, here's my take:

Small-bore Killing Power: With hits to vital areas and representative hunting loads						
Caliber	**Starling**	**Pigeon**	**Crow**	**Squirrel**	**Woodchuck**	**Fox**
.177 Airgun	DRT	Recov	Marginal	Marginal	NEG	—
.22 Airgun	DRT	DRT	Recov	Recov	NEG	—
.22 LR HVHP	DRT	DRT	DRT	DRT	Marginal	Marginal
.17 HMR	DRT	DRT	DRT	DRT	DRT	Recov
.22 WMR	DRT	DRT	DRT	DRT	DRT	DRT
Codes **DRT:** *Dead right there.* **NEG:** *Not enough gun.* ***Recov:*** *Recoverable. Quarry may travel a short distance.*						

The above opinions (that's all they are) are based on upper-body hits at reasonable distances. A head-shot woodchuck will be DRT with a .22 LR non-expanding round-nose bullet.

Chapter 4

A CLOSER LOOK AT RIFLES

With so many makes and models in circulation, it's hard to nail a final choice. This is especially true of .22 LR types, which have been in production since the late 1800s. Many have come and gone, but some, like the venerable Marlin Model 39 lever-action, are still going strong after more than a century. I wouldn't be afraid to buy a used rifle in decent shape if it falls within this category. Parts are always a concern, so it's reassuring to know that things like broken stocks or lost magazines can be replaced.

Since a properly chosen rimfire makes a nice centerfire training tool, common function shouldn't be overlooked. The choice you make here could guide you towards a nice, matching high-power rifle. Some readers will already have a favorite action type in mind, but others will be starting from scratch. The only real way to make sense out of things is to break the choices down by design or action classification. A good straightforward starting point is a universal type that continues to thrive after decades of steady use…

BOLT-ACTION RIFLES

Why would we consider a bolt-action rimfire survival gun? Well, besides the training quotient, it can be quietly used to harvest small game, leaving meat where a bigger bullet would just create a mess. A .22 LR will likely digest the whole gamut of cartridges, from high-speed Stingers to quiet CB Caps. The inherently strong action can also handle hotter calibers, like the .22 Magnum, for reasonable cost.

I'm not sure anyone could make an accurate guess as to the number of bolt-action rimfires in circulation today. The actual figure would be

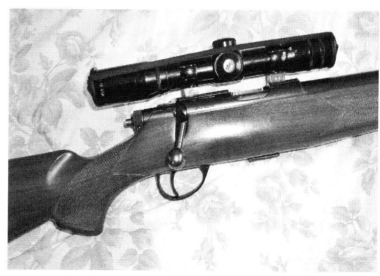

A no longer imported Chinese NS-522 bolt-action. It shoots great but good luck finding parts.

staggering, since the basic design has been in continuous production for well over a century. Many, no doubt, remain undiscovered in attics, basements, barns, and trunks. Prices range from several thousand dollars to less than a hundred, but the basic operation remains the same. Whether geared towards precise shooting or informal plinking, there really is something for everyone. With so many used guns in circulation, a basic but serviceable rifle can be purchased for peanuts.

New bolt-actions are available from a number of firms, many of which offer additional choices in the more potent calibers like .22 Magnum or .17 Hornady. There are rifles to match any budget, and those with deep pockets can drool over a selection of very high-end rifles like a Cooper. At the other end of the spectrum, lower-cost, domestically produced Marlin and Savage models are decent shooters. Both companies also offer higher-end but still affordable versions as well.

Factoring in both new and used options, listing everything would be difficult, if not impossible. For those on a shoestring budget, a trip through a well-stocked gun shop may hold hope of discovering a sturdy choice. Most will accommodate scope rings and as mentioned, many shoot surprisingly well.

Accuracy notes: When describing accuracy, you'll see the term "MOA". This stands for "minute of angle": a radial measurement equaling 1/60th of a degree. It coincidentally equals roughly one inch at 100 yards, or a half inch at 50 yards. One-MOA accuracy is considered "good".

AFFORDABLE DOMESTIC BOLT-ACTIONS

Browning T-Bolt: This old firm is headquartered in Utah, but their T-Bolt is actually built in Japan by Miroku. Browning is well known for quality firearms, and the latest "T-Bolt" is no exception. It's a modernized version of an older 1965 T-Bolt, but both share an interesting straight-pull action. In other words, retracting the bolt doesn't require lifting its handle.

Browning's latest T-Bolt, with a straight-pull action.

A central tang-mounted safety is similar to Browning's centerfire "A-bolt" rifles and their BPS pump shotguns. Another nice feature is a user-adjustable trigger. The new T-bolt uses an unusual "double helix" magazine, which holds 10 shots inside twin rotary compartments. The resulting trim, flush-fit design lends great handling qualities to this unique rifle. Several variations are offered in sporter or varmint-weight barrels, with wood or synthetic stocks. Calibers include .22 LR, .22 WMR, and .17 HMR. At less than five pounds, the synthetic versions are very lightweight. One useful feature is its stock compartment that holds a spare magazine. The "Green Reaper Suppressor Ready" .22 LR model has a threaded 16-inch barrel, offering some interesting possibilities.

The T-bolt's action isn't grooved, but is drilled and tapped. It accepts Weaver bases, which are included. They permit use of a huge assortment of scope rings in various heights, diameters and finishes. For any left-handed shooters, Browning has you covered. Although a bit different in function from their centerfire line, the T-bolt would make a nice small-bore choice.

Marlin: The company has been around for well over a century. Although I've used their lever-actions for many years, somehow their bolt-action rifles have evaded me. However, I know several folks who have used them, and they all share positive comments. For starters, the Marlins are affordable. I'm betting you could buy a perfectly adequate scope-equipped rifle for less than half the price of bare European offerings from Anschutz or Sako.

The Marlins are offered with tubular or detachable magazines, blued or stainless construction, and laminated or synthetic stocks. Caliber choices include .22 LR, .22 WRM, or .17 HMR. A youth-sized .22 is offered as a single-shot, or as a repeater capable of feeding Shorts, Longs, or Long Rifle cartridges.

Marlin's XT 22 SR bolt-action with Pro-fire trigger.

The "XT-Series" use Marlin's Pro-Fire Trigger, which is user-adjustable. It incorporates a center blade that prevents rearward movement unless fully depressed by the shooter's finger. A safe but light pull can thus be achieved. Marlin also builds their barrels using "Micro-Groove" rifling, which employs multiple small lands and grooves. In theory, accuracy is improved, but I discovered this system also provides slight improvement with shot loads. The so-called "rat-shot" cartridges contain a tiny payload of #12 shot, which some folks use on snakes or vermin. These loads won't cycle a semi-auto, making a bolt-action a better choice.

The Marlin bolt-actions are well thought out, widely distributed, and easy to maintain. A stainless steel version is a sensible, weatherproof choice if purchased with a synthetic stock. Their grooved receivers make scope mounting easy, too.

Remingtons, both older and newer: Oddly, Remington doesn't catalog any bolt-action rimfires at the moment, except for a very pricey Custom Shop Model 547. It's based on the recent Model 504, which appeared for a brief period several years ago. Prior to that, Remington produced numerous rimfire bolt-action rifles that remain in circulation as affordable used guns. Some are worth a look because there is little to go wrong. A good example is the Model 500 "Targetmaster" series. Remington made these .22 caliber rifles from 1939 through the early 1960s, producing more than a half million. Because they predate the 1968 Gun Control Act, serial numbers are absent. They're also usually bargain-priced. Both points will no doubt raise the interest of many readers.

I live in a rural area, and part of country living involves unwelcome creatures like red squirrels, skunks, and porcupines. Since they generally show up unannounced, a grab n' shoot solution can come in handy. In a longer barrel, standard-velocity .22 Shorts are *really* quiet, but hit with more force than so-called 'Magnum' airguns. My plan was to look for a cheap, used rifle that could remain on duty, outside the gun safe. A Remington Targetmaster seemed perfect. They were produced as single-shots, magazine, or tubular repeaters. I tracked down an old circa-1950 Model 510-X single-shot for $90 and gave it a thorough cleaning. Upon its purchase, I made sure it had a receiver with scope-mounting grooves because some of the earliest versions didn't. A basic Bushnell 4X rimfire scope was installed, and the whole package came in at less than $130.

The Author's old Remington M-510 single-shot bolt-action .22. Total cost was $130.

This little Remington shoots .22 Shorts with reasonable accuracy and, sure enough, its 24-inch barrel really quiets the report. The tiny rounds are easy to load: instead of inserting them into the chamber, I just toss them in its single-shot receiver and close the bolt. At 25 yards, accuracy is useful with .22 Shorts. Using .22 LR Federal Gold Medal Target, it puts five shots in 5/8" at 50 yards – darned good accuracy from any rifle!

The M-510's small dimensions and basic operation also make it a good trainer for younger shooters. The chamber is clearly visible when the bolt is rearward, and the simple design is easy to master. With good ammo, it shoots nearly as well as my Anschutz M-1416 D-HB, which cost ten times as much!

Somehow, I've managed to own a fair assortment of other Remington bolt-actions, most of which have since been traded off. They dated from the 1960s up through present times, and all, save one, were very good shooters. The exception was a Model 541T HB that is known as a real ringer. Mine was too, but not until several shots warmed up its barrel. As no stranger to accuracy improvements, I tried just about everything to no avail. The other older Remingtons I've sampled shot somewhere north of ½" at 50 yards without much testing.

As a Remington Model 700 centerfire aficionado, I look for rimfire models with similar function, particularly in the safety switch location. When Remington came out with their Model 504, I snapped one up in .22 LR. It feels and operates much like its larger M-700 centerfire cousin. I wish it shot as well, but this was not to be. The barrel attachment and stock bedding juncture is a bit unorthodox. I've tinkered with it, using shims to wring out better groups. Doing some research, I found a detailed description of an effective glass bedding process specific to this rifle. By dumb luck, I ran into the author at a gun show. He claimed phenomenal improvement and offered a hand, which I've yet to find time for. Meanwhile, it's shooting under ¾" at 50 yards with Remington .22 LR Subsonic Hollow-points. I use it to practice off-hand shooting on four-inch steel knock-down plates, and it's also my preferred squirrel rifle, nicely complementing the full-size Remington Model 700s. My son picked up a used heavy-barreled Model 504 in .17 HMR. It's no flyweight, but like most other .17s, it certainly shoots more accurately than my .22 LR. Sadly, the M-504s are now discontinued, except for the surviving and expensive Custom Shop Model 547 version. I mention these rifles because of the upcoming centerfire manual. It contains an M-700 centerfire recommendation, which the M-504 closely mimics.

Remington's M-504 .22, a nice companion to their popular M-700 centerfire.

Ironically, the older and more spartan rifles like my Model 510 have proven plenty accurate. With so many in circulation, parts can still be found. In fact, if need be, an entire replacement rifle could be bought for a very reasonable cost. Parts for the newer M-504 will be difficult to locate, and extra magazines have pretty much dried up. The lesson here is that established systems do have value.

Ruger: The Model 77 rimfire series includes a broad line of good rifles. They're very solidly built and operate like their larger, centerfire Model 77 cousins. It's been a while since I used a Model 77-22, but the recent rifles appear unchanged. Having used .22 LR, .22 WMR, and .17 HMR versions, they all produced excellent results. The rifles are built like tanks and use Ruger's solid scope-mounting system. Their rotary magazines hold plenty of ammo, but sit flush and work reliably. For anyone considering the .308 Model 77 Scout Rifle, a rimfire counterpart would make a whole lot of sense. The safety operates similarly to the famous Winchester Model 70's, too.

The solidly-built Ruger Model 77/22, available in several calibers and configurations.

I have some experience with two different .22 Magnum Rugers: a blued, walnut version and a stainless, laminated rifle. Both shot right around one MOA, meaning they would reliably put five shots inside an inch at 100 yards. My lead instructor has a stainless/laminated .17 HMR that shoots as well as my Anschutz, for less money. It'll stay under 1 MOA.

While the M-77 series is well-established, a brand new rifle has just appeared. It's a rimfire twin to Ruger's "American" centerfire series, and has a number of *very* appealing features, including an affordable price. Full size and compact models are offered. The stocks are cleverly designed with interchangeable cheek-piece modules. The "American Rimfire" looks like a real winner. Of course, being new, it has no established track record or widespread source for parts. However, it is produced by a solid company. Rifles in .22 LR, .22 WMRF, and .17 HMR are available, all of which use Ruger's existing rotary magazines. The .22 LR American uses the common 10/22 type and, since that model has been a top seller for 50 years, magazines are everywhere.

Ruger's affordable new "American" is an adaptive design that covers all bases.

Savage: Here's another firm with a well-developed rimfire line. I've read many positive reports about their accuracy, and the examples I tried backed up these claims. You get a good, honest rifle for a fair price. The lower-cost rifles include a neat little single-shot youth version called the "Rascal". A slightly larger Mark II repeater is also offered, along with adult-sized rifles. At the upper end of their line is the Tactical model, which emulates a high-powered sniper rifle. Another has a laminated, thumbhole stock with exotic colors. The barrel is spiral-fluted, and the visual aspect is attention-getting. Most are available with the very innovative "Accu-Trigger" that safely permits light adjustments. It's a blade-within-trigger design that other rifle manufacturers now emulate.

The affordable but great-shooting Savage MKII SSF, with an Accu-Trigger.

Threaded muzzles are offered on a few models as well. As mentioned previously, with .22 Shorts or lower-powered CB Caps, in a longer-barreled rifle their report is almost undetectable. For more thump, .22 Long Rifle subsonic loads are available. They're fairly quiet because they lack the sonic crack of high-velocity .22 LR rounds. A bolt-action's breech remains sealed after the shot, so all the noise goes out the muzzle. If a suppressor (or so-called silencer) is installed, subsonic rounds are very stealthy. Threaded muzzles are offered just for this purpose.

The Savage rimfire rifles are laid out similarly to Marlins. Both firms offer centerfire rifles and their small-bores make nice matches. The safeties are also similar to Remington's design, meaning they'll serve well as an understudy trainer. However, Savage has left-handed shooters covered as well. That's not too common with rimfire rifles, especially among lower cost models.

EUROPEAN BOLT-ACTIONS

For those with deeper pockets, several tantalizing rifles beckon. They are darn good rifles, but less common than domestic models. Prospective buyers should invest in at least one spare magazine.

The Anschutz M-64s: This German firm is well known for their excellent Olympic-grade .22 target rifles. Most are built on the precise and costly M-54 action, which is also the basis for some sporters. Anschutz sells another line of rifles built on their simpler and less expensive Model 64 action. I've had good luck with several.

Two presently in use are a .22 LR Model 1416D HB and a .17 HMR Model 1517. Both are based on the lower-priced but serviceable magazine-fed M-64. "Lower-priced" is subjective, since neither is really cheap. The safeties are side-mounted behind the bolts, in positions relevant to my Model 700s. The triggers are adjustable, but both were great right out of their boxes. Both bolt knobs are oversized. Anschutz uses the wider European 11mm receiver scope-mounting grooves that can cause fitting issues with some American rings. I have Millett 1" rings on both rifles, and they worked without any problems. Why spend a bunch of money on a lowly .22? Because it's part of a bigger picture and can play a key part.

The Anschutz .22 LR Model 1516 is based on the M-64 action. The safety is located similarly to a Remington centerfire M-700. The scope rings are from Millet.

My .22 LR Anschutz has a medium/heavy barrel contour. It's set up as a precision trainer, augmenting larger caliber, heavy-barreled rifles. A Burris 4x12 AO Rimfire/Airgun Scope with a parallax-correcting adjustable objective (AO) lens was mounted (see the scope section for more information). I installed QD sling swivel studs, with a second in the wide beavertail forend for bipod attachment. Paintballs perched on golf tees make great 50-yard prone targets, scaled to centerfire golf-balls at 100 yards or more. The distances don't need to be exact, and can be adjusted to one's personal limitations.

Anschutz triggers are adjustable but this one was great, right out of the box.

A pair of Anschutz rimfires built on the M-64 action. M-1514 D-HB .22 LR (top); and M-1517 in .17 HMR.

The .17 HMR Anschutz has a medium/heavy sporting-weight barrel and factory-installed sling studs. It is set up for field use, and this one has seen plenty! Among the several guns I'd hate to be without, a .17 HMR is near the top of the list. For those living west of The Big Muddy where ranges run long, it might not have as much value. However, this rifle has made two trips there for à la carte use on prairie dogs. Both expeditions were highly entertaining, and the Model 1517 saw plenty of action. Mine has accounted for lots of crows and other varmints, using an older Leupold VX-2 4x12 AO scope. The power selector pretty much stays parked at 8X, with the adjustable objective set for 100 yards. One day I may switch to something with a holdover reticle just to stretch its range a bit, but for now, I'm happy with the knowledge that anything inside 130 yards is in serious trouble. Plenty of hits have happened well beyond this distance, but wind is a real factor with .17 HMR flyweight bullets.

Two quirks pertaining to the Anschutz M-64 action involve bolt-knob related misfires and occasional ejection hang-ups. I've learned to spot-check my bolts to make sure they are fully seated. The large knobs permit easy operation with gloved hands, but can be inadvertently nudged upwards a bit. If that happens, you'll hear a click instead of a bang. It's really not a huge problem once you understand the cause. Others have reported intermittent, incomplete ejection of .22 LR fired brass. Mine has a minor hang-up now and then, but overall, it works well.

When you buy an Anschutz, you'll get a known quantity, which is predictably very good. Having struggled with a pile of other rifles in search of true MOA accuracy, I have no regrets. But they ain't cheap!

CZ Rimfires: While we're on European rifles, the CZ line deserves a look. By most accounts, the Czech-built rimfires are great shooters, at prices *well* below the German rifles. They are solidly made from machined steel and walnut, along with synthetic-stocked versions. I'm not too keen on the bolt-mounted safety, but in all fairness, it is very positive (clearly, I have a safety fetish issue).

CZ recently changed their barrel-mounting system, and they now advertise interchangeable calibers from just one action. The action needs to be unscrewed from the stock to access cap screws, which are then backed out for barrel swaps. One receiver will accept all four popular rimfire calibers, which may be of interest to some. A scope re-zero would probably be necessary since it remains mounted to the receiver. Among their many models, CZ also sells a nice junior model. The CZ "American" is an elegant little rifle with classic lines, and can be purchased with a walnut or synthetic stock. A friend owns a stubby 16-inch .22 LR with a threaded muzzle. He says he's shot phenomenal groups averaging well below one MOA. Considering what he paid, I'm extremely jealous. Left-handed shooters haven't been ignored, either.

The CZ Model 455 American is a great shooter at a very fair price.

Their reasonable prices make CZ rifles great picks for those who appreciate solidly built examples of old-school design.

Sako: This Finland-based firm is known for high quality rifles, and Sako (pronounced "sock-o") is now a subsidiary of Beretta. Sako rimfire bolt-actions have come and gone over the years, but all were known as great shooters. I once owned a collection of Sakos, including a .22 LR Model 78 bolt-action. It shot wonderfully right out of the box, and I still regret selling it.

However, the latest "Finfire II" and "Quad" models have taken up the slack. The Finfire II is a follow-up to the previous version, which was known for its exceptional accuracy. It has classic lines and is chambered for .22 LR or .17 HMR, both of which employ a detachable magazine. The similar Quad series has been in production for a while, and offers interchangeable barrels in .22LR, .22 WMR, .17 HMR, and .17 Mach 2. Each barrel has a color-coded band that corresponds with a matching pair of magazines for quick identification. Sako claims zero will remain constant between barrel changes, due to tight tolerances. Still, separate scope adjustments will likely be necessary for each caliber.

Sako's classy switch-barrel "Quad" permits use of four different rimfire calibers.

Several versions are offered, including the "Hunter Pro", which emulates Sako's centerfire Model 75. Also sold is a varmint-weight rifle, an intriguing heavy-barreled "Range" bench-type affair. A synthetic stock is another, practical option.

Other bolt-action rifles: The Sako rifles are a Mercedes rimfire offering, which is also true of the Anschutz line. The same can be said for the U.S.-built Cooper rifles, which are a rung higher in stature. Ultra Light Arms is another small company offering an intriguing and precise rifle. They're not for everyone, and will mostly appeal to serious gun nuts.

Others will view a rimfire rifle as an accessory that fills a useful slot in their gun safe. I've really only touched on the available choices. Earlier, I mentioned the beginning of my rimfire odyssey, which involved a shiny new Mossberg Model 320 K. This firm was a strong force in the 1960 rimfire market, selling a diverse line of rifles. Well, things have changed. They still list .22 rifles, but their bolt-actions are labeled "International", indicating offshore production. Perhaps the most iconic rifle manufacturer is Winchester. A large assortment of rimfire rifles left their plant, starting in the 19th Century. They have since disappeared, but still show up as used guns.

Bolt-action pros and cons: A design that can handle various calibers is a good thing. As we advance from the .22 Long Rifle to the .22 Winchester Magnum Rimfire, rifle choices diminish. The .22 WMR has more power and has been problematic in some semi-automatic rifles. The same holds true for the .17 Hornady Magnum Rimfire and smaller .17 Mach 2. The bolt-action is the perfect platform for these rimfire loads and most can achieve surprising accuracy.

Most of the U.S.-made rifles we covered have been in continuous production for many years. Odds are good that you'll never have a problem, but if you do, parts will be available. That's something to keep in mind, especially when using a detachable-magazine design. Legions of older rifles with missing magazines sit idle for want of this key piece. The design is also simple to maintain since just about all have an easily removable bolt. Brush off the bolt's face, run a rod through the breech, and you're done. Many other action types eventually quit, mainly because their owners don't know how to service them!

There are two bolt-action downsides, which won't affect everyone. The first involves new shooters and single-shot rifles. They certainly are a safe and logical choice, but from a training perspective, single-shots can also hinder future proficiency. My sons, who are experienced hunters, can really run a bolt gun. In the woods, their follow-up shots sound more like semi-auto fire. This skill has rescued a shaky situation and filled our freezers on more than one occasion. They're programmed to run their bolts with mounted rifles, thanks to early rimfire training. They started with .22 bolt-action repeaters and began by loading just one round. Later, they advanced to pairs and then triples. Those learning exclusively on single shots will soon develop an ingrained habit of dismounting any repeater between shots. It's a hard habit to break.

The second issue involves left-handed shooters, who really need a rifle with the bolt on its port side. Choices are fairly limited, something to keep in mind from a training point of view. Based on cost, a Savage will become a viable choice.

Balancing expense against everything mentioned above, plus survival-oriented features like stainless steel construction and synthetic or laminated stocks, both Marlin and Savage really stand out. They're widely distributed and available in offerings to suit most budgets. The receivers are grooved for easy scope mounting, and their accuracy warrants optics.

However, the brand new Ruger American may eventually eclipse everything. It just looks like one hell of a rifle, comparing its features against the price!

Whether high-end, economy priced, new or used, there really is a bolt-action for just about everyone.

SEMI-AUTOMATICS – NON-MAGNUM

It's probably safe to say that more rifles in this category are sold today than any other type. Once loaded, a shot can be fired with each squeeze of the trigger. Most use a basic blowback design, whereby a breech bolt is cycled due to discharge force. Without the need for a more elaborate gas-metered system, cost is reasonable compared to centerfire models. Positive function is achieved through a balance of recoil, bolt mass, and springs, so ammunition choices may narrow somewhat. Just about all are set up for .22 LR, and marked accordingly. Browning, Marlin, and Ruger offer takedown models for quick disassembly and compact storage.

Browning: John Browning's renowned .22 Automatic has been in production since 1913, claiming the honor of the longest running rimfire auto-loader. It has a barrel nut that can be unscrewed to separate the rifle for storage. The later models use a barrel-mounted scope base, which extends rearward over the receiver. The system maintains zero, since the scope is mounted to the barrel. Despite its small size and detachable barrel, the Browning actually shoots fairly accurately. It is a trim little rifle, which feeds rounds through a tubular magazine located in the stock. I've always felt that this design is safer than barrel-mounted magazines, because the shooter's hands never get near the muzzle during loading.

Browning's timeless Semi-Auto .22 feeds from a tubular magazine located within its stock. It quickly disassembles for compact storage..

Browning also sells a somewhat strange adaptation of their "Buckmark" pistol. I do have some experience with that firearm, and consider it an excellent choice. Their rifle is pretty much the same gun with two stock connecting points at its rear. The result is a somewhat odd-looking but racy carbine.

The modern Buckmark .22 semi-automatic rifle is based on Browning's excellent pistol. It shares similar features and feeds from a detachable magazine.

Henry: Although mainly known for their line of U.S.-made lever-actions, this U.S. firm now offers a reincarnated clip-fed AR-7 survival rifle that was an off-again, on-again product, originally produced through Armalite for emergency use by Air Force pilots. This fly-weight semi-auto .22 LR refuses to die after 50+ years because of its innovative features. The barrel/receiver assembly can be easily separated and stowed inside a hollow plastic ABS stock. The resulting package is barely 16 inches long, and weighs but 3 ½ pounds thanks to aluminum construction. A simple nut quickly connects the barreled action to the stock without tools. Henry has tweaked the design and now sells it as the "U.S. Survival AR-7". Their new Teflon finish stands up well to bad weather, and the Henry version has a grooved receiver. Many users will no doubt stick with the factory peep sight arrangement, but a scope mounting option is always a nice touch. So is the pair of 8-shot magazines included with each Henry. It's not a match grade rifle, but the AR-7's accuracy is perfectly adequate for its intended use. The "Survival" moniker says it all, and cost is fairly reasonable.

The take-down Henry AR-7 disassembles in seconds. Its barreled .22 LR action stows in the stock.

Marlin: Marlin offers tubular and detachable magazine .22 LR models, in blued or stainless steel. Those sold today are based on the well-designed Model 60 action. The M-795 rifles are just magazine-fed M-60 variations.

Like many shooters, I tend to focus heavily on optics (bad pun). Once in a while, though, it's fun to do some good old-fashioned iron sight plinking. I spied a stainless steel Marlin Model 60 on sale with a blue laminated stock and tubular magazine. It seemed like a good choice for high-volume shooting with its 14+1 capacity. I had previously owned a clip-fed Model 795, which ran reliably but required frequent reloads.

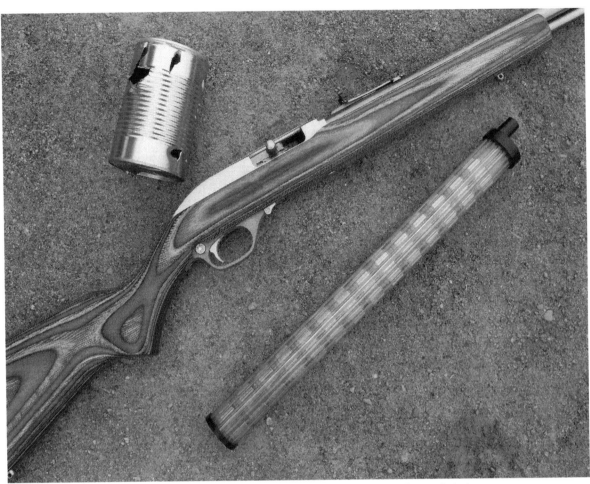

Marlin's Model 60 .22 LR with a Spee-D-Loader and perforated victim.

The Model 60 has been around for years. As it turns out, this one is surprisingly accurate, even with iron sights. It's one of the few rifles I've owned that never saw an optical sight. Shooting match ammo off bags, 25-yard groups hovered right around ½-inch. The trigger was heavy, which is where the Internet comes in. After a bit of research, I tweaked a spring, which helped. Then I swapped out the front blade for a green fiber-optic bead, and proceeded to squirt some lead downrange. While loading a tubular magazine can be time-consuming, it's pretty darned easy to empty one! The remedy is a very handy gadget called a "Spee-D-Loader". It's a clear, plastic cylinder with 8 internal tubes and a rotating cap that has a single spout. Each tube holds up to 15 .22 LR rounds for a total capacity of 120 rounds. You just twist the cap until the spout aligns with a column and pour its contents into your magazine. When not in use, you can park the cap so it doesn't align with the ammo reservoirs. The Marlin's magazine holds 14 rounds, so I fill each loading tube with that amount of ammo.

The rifle has one feature I really like: it locks open on the last shot. That's the cue to reload. The captured bolt also prevents dry-fires, which can eventually damage the chamber mouth of many rimfires. I keep the Spee-D-Loader pre-filled to save time on the range. The Marlin is great fun on close-quarter action targets like metal spinners or tossed cans.

A couple of cautions apply to tubular magazines. First, they're harder to visually clear. Secondly, for those models (like the Marlin) with barrel-mounted magazines, extra care is necessary during loading. Your fingers are near the business end, so that task requires extra attention. The Marlin is a solid workhorse rifle, if somewhat more pedestrian than the Ruger 10/22. Aftermarket accessories do exist, but choices are much more limited. If money is an issue, the Model 60, 795, or takedown Papoose are all worth a look.

Remington: The Model 552 Speedmaster is somewhat unique because it will fire .22 Long Rifle, Longs, or Shorts interchangeably. It uses a tubular magazine, hung under the barrel. The receiver is grooved for a scope, and also has a small protruding brass deflector that left-handed shooters may appreciate. The safety is located behind the trigger guard, in the same location as Remington's Model 870 shotgun and their other semi-auto firearms. The button can be reversed for left-handed use. The M-552 has been built in various grades over the years, from plain models to the latest checkered BDL model. It would nicely compliment a Remington centerfire autoloader.

Remington's Model 552 Speedmaster feeds .22 Shorts, Longs, or Long Rifle cartridges interchangeably.

The newer Model 597 was introduced in 1997. It is Remington's answer to the Ruger 10/22, and even has a similar appearance. One big improvement over the 10/22 is a last shot bolt-lock feature. The M-597 has been offered in .22 LR, .22 WMR, and .17 HMR. The latter round was problematic and has been discontinued. The .22 LR version feeds from a detachable 10-shotbox magazine. You can still buy a .22 WMR, which is heavier and uses an 8-shot magazine. Various M-597 versions have been offered with different barrel lengths and stocks. The receivers are grooved, and also tapped for a one-piece Weaver scope base.

A base-line Remington M-597, chambered for .22 Long Rifle.

Although no longer in production, the Nylon-66 is another neat little rifle. It appeared in the 1950s as a 15-shot, lightweight .22 LR that employed a one-piece "Zytel" nylon stock. The "receiver" was really just a metal shroud to help minimize weight and provide scope grooves. The tang safety was located behind it and on top. The rifle fed from a tubular magazine housed within the butt plate. Lately, the M-66 is becoming somewhat collectable, but enough were made to increase odds of stumbling on to a deal. Overall, the M-66 is a simple little rifle that works and shoots reasonably well. We still have an "Apache Black" version with a nickel-plated receiver that has been going strong since 1970.

Ruger's hugely popular 10-22 carbine in basic form.

Ruger: Among the most popular rifles is the 10/22, which has a detachable rotary 10-round magazine. The takedown Ruger is the latest offering, with a slightly different and extremely convenient disassembly process. Again, the rifle is a stainless/synthetic design sold with a handy storage case.

What really sets the Ruger apart is its modular design. Several factory models are available, from basic birch-stocked rifles to a heavy barreled target version. For those seeking the ultimate rifle, the sky is the limit. Any hobbyist can switch out barrels, stocks, and trigger assemblies right on the kitchen table. A large amount of interesting aftermarket accessories are readily available, permitting true customization. Several firms like Volquartsen produce high-end components, including proprietary match trigger assemblies, precision receivers, and match barrels. When complimented with good optics, decent accuracy is possible.

Not that the factory-issued version is bad. It isn't, and most will shoot decent groups. Still, the quest for tack-driving accuracy, combined with ease of installation, will always ensure a supply of interesting aftermarket trinkets. My 10/22 started with a Ruger receiver, to which a VQ heavy stainless compensated barrel and a Brown Precision stock are fastened. A Power scope base accepts Warne QD scope rings, which repeat zero. Two ring sets permit use of different optical sights. For precise shooting, a scope is used. Fast and furious close-range work involves a separate 30 mm dot sight. Several extra 10-shot magazines complete the package, providing a very nifty setup.

The Author's customized Ruger 10/22 with aftermarket stock and barrel.

The one gripe I have with a 10/22 is that the bolt won't lock open on the last shot. You can manually latch it to the rear, but as the British say, it's "fiddly". Of course, when it comes to the Ruger, you can bet someone is always working on a way to make it better. A lockback system is available, but requires specially modified magazines. Improved bolt latches are out there, too. You might want to sit on your wallet, because it would be easy to blow a grand on a custom 10/22. For our purposes, factoring in fair value, weather resistance, and utility, the takedown model would be a good choice. The latest version has a threaded muzzle, offering interesting suppressor possibilities.

AR-15 .22 conversion units and clones: The latest trend involves AR-15 rimfire knock-offs. The process began years ago with modified, drop-in AR-15 bolt carrier assemblies and special magazines. These conversion units permitted the use of high-speed, .22 LR ammunition in a standard AR-15 .223. The latter's bore diameter is a tad larger than the former's, resulting in so-so accuracy. Lead fouling in gas tubes was another reported problem. Finally, a few firms began offering dedicated rimfire upper receivers, and both options are still available.

AR-15 .22 LR conversion kit. Note the modified magazine.

An AR-15 .22 LR conversion kit, ready for drop-in installation.

Next came complete AR-15 rimfire rifle clones. Some were cosmetic representations based on more conventional models, but when Smith & Wesson introduced their AR .22 rimfire rifle, a new chapter dawned. The S&W M&P 15-22 is mostly plastic, but shares some common AR-15 parts. Function is identical to a standard AR-15, and price is fairly reasonable. Picking one up, an immediate revelation as a long-time AR-15 shooter was that running the S&W .22 was old hat.

S&W's rimfire clone will be immediately familiar to any AR-15 or M-16 users.

Many, but not all parts will interchange with AR-15 components. Stocks, pistol grips, and triggers are supposedly common, but the receiver halves are intentionally different. Disassembly is, however, fairly similar. Both push pins are there, and cleaning is a breeze. Pushing the rear pin allows the receiver halves to separate. The charging handle (plastic) and bolt assembly can be withdrawn just like an AR-15, but the rimfire lacks a gas system and is easier to maintain. Push the front pin and you have a true takedown rifle. Unable to resist, I took the plunge.

An early production S&W M&P 15-22 with dot-sight and light.

The forend/quad rails provide plenty of mounting points. The supplied sights are just fine, but my S&W AR-22 is wearing an inexpensive Walther dot sight that seems perfect on this rifle. I did mount a low-powered 1.75x5 scope in order to do some accuracy testing. Actually, I've owned two AR-22s. The first rifle, an early specimen, was nothing special. It had a basic G.I. telescoping stock and bare muzzle. Accuracy was mediocre. I sold it to fund a later model that had a few factory improvements.

Later model S&W MOE .22 LR, set up for accuracy testing.

Initial test 25-yard results. Subsequent 50-yard testing with Federal Gold Medal Target (right target) was roughly the same.

My second S&W M&P 15-22 is an MOE Model. It has a Magpul collapsible stock and pistol grip, plus a threaded muzzle with an A-2 flash-cage. Although far from match grade, it shoots reasonably well. Federal bulk-pack HVHPs run without a hitch, grouping under 1.5" at 50 yards. Federal Gold Medal Target puts 5 shots into roughly one inch at the same distance. Groups with the earlier S&W were around twice that size.

Here's one thing to consider, though. A high sighting system makes close range hits difficult. Rounds will strike noticeably low by an error equivalent to the distance between bore and sight centerlines. For small game hunting, this can be a problem. On the other hand, an AR-type .22 is lots of fun to shoot! I would probably not have included this rifle if interest in AR-15 type firearms wasn't so strong. For any such fans, I'd rate the S&W M&P 15-22 as a rifle worth owning.

MAGNUM SEMI-AUTOMATICS

I've broken these rifles out into a separate category because they vary in design. Their increased power requires re-engineering to properly control bolt velocity and pressure. A conventional blowback action won't work, and modifications can produce a rifle that handles differently.

For whatever reason, .22 WMR semi-autos tend to come and go. Part of the problem may involve the design challenges associated with the hotter round. Perhaps this issue was a factor in the disappearance of Ruger's interesting .22 Magnum version of their 10/22. The only rimfire Magnum semi-auto I ever owned was an H&K Model 300, chambered for .22 WMR. It was an interesting rifle, but in typical Teutonic fashion, was over-engineered. Price for a used one today would be through the roof.

CZ: Sells an interesting new .22 WMR that feeds from a detachable 5-shot magazine. Unlike their bolt-actions, this rifle utilizes a fair amount of polymer. The receiver is partially made out of this material, although its butt stock and forend are wood. The result is a handsome rifle of conventional appearance, with fairly light weight.

CZ's latest magazine-fed Model 512 is chambered for .22 WMR.

Magnum Research: These 10/22-based rifles resemble Rugers, but are internally quite different, employing a hybrid gas/blowback design. Much emphasis is placed on their lightweight alloy construction, including small-diameter steel barrels wrapped with carbon fiber. MR warns against use of lighter .22 WMR bullets, so owners will need to stick with weights of 40–50 grains.

MRI's .22 WMR looks like a Ruger 10/22, but has internal differences. Its carbon-fiber barrel greatly reduces weight.

Remington: The Model 597 .22 WMR employs a heavy tungsten bolt to delay blowback, which also raises cost compared to the .22 LR model. The Magnum version is somewhat large but manageable. A friend's now discontinued version looks really sharp with its laminated stock and stainless barreled action. It's also surprisingly accurate. The M-597s locks open on the last shot, which, for me, is a desirable trait. Somewhat interestingly, Remington abandoned production of a .17 HMR version due to pressure issues related to that cartridge.

A Remington Model 597 LS HB, chambered for .22 WMR.

Volquartsen: I have a good friend who owned a heavy-barreled .22 WMR, which is a high-end and very expensive semi-custom 10/22 facsimile. It shot very accurately, which came as no surprise, considering the excellent reputation of Volquartsen Custom. VQ conquered function challenges with an internal counterweight, selling both .17 HMR and .22 WMR rifles. They weigh a full half pound more than their rimfire progeny, and either one will set you back a grand or more. Anyone looking for the ultimate Magnum should save their pennies for a Volquartsen rifle. Several versions are available.

The majestic .22 WMR Volquartsen Deluxe Sporter shoots as well as it looks!

I like the idea of a semi-automatic .22 Magnum rifle. You get a lot more punch and range than you would with any .22 Long Rifle, but the report is still fairly mild. As a hand-loader, I'm always chasing brass, and the disposable .22 WMR casings nicely cure this addiction. A Magnum Research or Volquartsen rifle would nicely compliment a Ruger .22 LR Model 10/22. In fact, both firms also market their own .22 LR versions of this rifle.

SLIDE ACTION (OR PUMP) RIFLES

The glory days of the once popular shooting gallery guns have waned. Semi-autos rule the roost, so new pump guns are slim pickings.

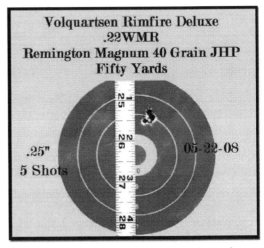

The proof is in the pudding. No surprises here, thanks to Volquartsen quality.

Remington Model 572: The "Fieldmaster" continues to sell after decades of production. It feeds .22 Shorts, Longs, and Long Rifle ammunition interchangeably from a tubular magazine. It looks much like their .22 semi-auto, with the same safety, side ejection, and a grooved receiver.

The Remington pump would make a great component of the three-gun system described in *Survival Guns: A Beginner's Guide*. As described, it would match up nicely with a Remington Model 870 shotgun and Model 760 centerfire rifle. In other words, you'd gain a perfect trainer. The rimfire version isn't cheap, costing much more than their basic "Express" shotgun. However, some of that cost could be amortized through use of lower-cost .22 LR ammunition geared towards practice.

The Remington Model 572 Fieldmaster pump will eat just about any type of .22 ammo. It also runs like Remington's M-870 shotguns and M-760 centerfire rifles.

I owned a Remington M-572, mainly because it would handle .22 Shorts. In fact, I bought it used just for that purpose. The previous owner claimed it would shoot them extremely well, and he was right. I used it to practice on hand-thrown targets, since the range of a .22 Short is…well, short. It was eventually sold because I'm not a pump gun fan, but truthfully, that decision was really a mistake. Following my own advice, I should have kept it and added two more slide actions - a shotgun and centerfire rifle. So, of course, I didn't.

Henry: This U.S. firm lists a pump reminiscent of a gallery rifle, complete with octagonal barrel and corncob forend. Unlike some of the old-time rifles, this modernized version ejects through the side of the receiver, meaning its top will accept a scope. Two models are offered: a .22 LR and a .22 Magnum.

Henry's pump-action rifle is well-built gun, available in both .22 LR and .22 WMR.

LEVER-ACTION RIFLES

The all-American rifle continues to thrive. While nostalgia plays a part, the main reason for the lev-ergun's longevity is simple. After a century and a half of steady use, the design still works. In truth, we might consider it the original assault rifle. In fact, "that damn Yankee rifle you loaded on Sunday and fired all week" was a rimfire, although one chambered for a larger .44 bullet. I've owned several rimfire lever-actions built by Marlin, Browning, and Winchester. They were quality rifles, but there are others worth a look.

Marlin: During the late 1800s, Marlin hit upon a winner with the .22 Model 1891, which has mor-phed (with only minor changes) into the Model 39A. It remains the oldest shoulder-fired gun in continuous production, and is still a great pick today. There have been several Model 39 variations, from straight-hand stocked carbines to pistol grip stocked rifles. They all share a common receiver, machined from solid steel. A knurled takedown knob on its right side can be unscrewed with a coin, permitting disassembly for storage or maintenance. The best way to clean a barrel is from breech to muzzle, which is possible with a Model 39 (watch out for the loose ejector that will fall free). Marlin still touts their "Micro-Groove" rifling, which employs 16 fine lands and grooves. I'm not sure if it makes a major difference in accuracy, but this design does seem to slightly improve rat-shot patterns.

Marlins feed just about everything, and hold plenty of .22 Long Rifle, Long, or Short cartridges that are housed in a tubular magazine hung under its barrel. A supplied hammer extension provides better access when a scope is mounted, although the receiver top isn't grooved. It is tapped for in-expensive scope bases, a common type being Weaver's one-piece rail. My old M-39 still sits within reach, going strong after being purchased as a used rifle sometime during the early 1970s. Although I like scopes, this one sports a Lyman receiver sight and green fiber-optic front bead. The aperture has been removed from the Lyman peep, permitting a ghost-ring sight picture. It's fast to line up, works great in the woods, and does reasonably well in low light. Marlin's M-39 is a classic, solidly-built rifle that complements their centerfire offerings. The current Model 39A Golden is a full-size rifle with a 24-inch barrel. Its magazine capacity is humongous, holding 19 .22 LRs or 26 Shorts! The walnut stock has a pistol grip and is checkered. Marlin lists its weight at around 6 ½ pounds, which is certainly manageable.

Marlin's well-proven take-down Model 39-A Golden holds lots of ammo. It would nicely compliment one of their centerfire lever-guns.

Browning: The same firm that sells the T-Bolt also builds a novel rack-and-pinion version of their centerfire BLR. Like its centerfire brother, the rimfire lever-action is a well-made rifle available in several grades. These unique leverguns run off a short 33-degree lever throw, which also contains the trigger. The .22 would make a great companion piece, and at one time I owned both, the first being a floral engraved Grade II BL-22, chambered in .22 LR. It was easy to scope thanks to the grooved receiver, and the whole package was very handy in the woods. Accuracy was useful, and its function nicely complemented my centerfire .358 Winchester BLR big game rifle. A BL-22 won't hurt your eyes one bit. The higher grade is just window dressing, and a Grade I will serve admirably. Like the other lever-action rimfires, the Browning BL-22 has an external hammer, and feeds from a tubular magazine that will feed 15 .22 LR rounds, as well as Long or Short cartridges. A shorter youth-sized "Micro" version holds 11 shots and weighs less than five pounds. A fancy, full-sized octagonal-barrel model is another option that really catches my eye. Regardless of the model, a BL-22 is a slim and handy rifle, even when matched with a low-magnification scope like a 4X type. As far as I know, the BL-22s don't have sling studs, but they can always be installed.

The Browning BL-22 is a classy short-stroke lever-action that employs a unique rack & pinion design. Their similar centerfire BLR can digest modern cartridges, providing an appealing two-gun system.

Henry: I don't have any personal experience with the modern production Henrys, but they do have plenty of fans. They employ classic styling and greatly resemble the now discontinued Winchester Model 9422 lever-actions that were marketed towards centerfire Model 94 owners. For the millions of owners still prowling the woods with their trusty .30/30s, a small-bore Henry becomes a logical choice. Numerous variations are sold, ranging from Henry's basic model through ornate commemorative examples. Like the Marlin and Browning rifles, a Henry will feed all .22 ammo types, from LR to Shorts. A very compact youth model is sold, along with some other intriguing spinoffs. Henry's .22 WMR holds 12 total rounds that are launched from a 19 ¼" barrel – a length sufficient for generating decent velocity. This rifle weighs just over 5 ¼ pounds, and its receiver is grooved for scope mounting. Adding one will still result in a portable package, great for pounding around the outdoors. Henry posts a 50-yard accuracy claim of 5 .22 WMR shots inside one inch, which is certainly useable performance. Another variant is chambered for the .17 HMR. One great feature is a higher stock for use with a scope – something this flat-shooting caliber deserves. But just in case iron sights are called for, Henry has you covered. The .17 model also sports highly visible fiber-optic open Williams Fire Sights. The distinct and separate "Frontier" series is fitted with 20-inch octagonal barrels that impart a classic western image. Iron sights are standard, and the Frontier is listed in .22LR, .22 WMR, or .17 HMR calibers. These rifles are proudly advertised as "built in the USA", and they're reasonably priced to boot.

The handsome Henry "Classic" is but one of many good-shooting models.

Mossberg: For those who can't decide if they're 19th century cowboys or 21st century tactical operators, Mossberg offers a real grabber. It's their Model SPX lever-action, which resembles the culmination of a Winchester or Henry .22 that's been thrown in a blender with an M4/AR-15 carbine. The result is something with lots of Picatinny rails, a telescoping stock, and a lever. You'll probably either love it or hate it. I suppose it makes sense for anyone contemplating Mossberg's similar centerfire .30/30 package. Actually, I've long bemused the public's infatuation with any sort of black rifle sporting such protuberances. We've seen some very capable shooters who could whoop most tactical fanciers with nothing more than an old-time levergun. Well, here's a chance to meld the old with the new, while adding some mounting points for lights, mudflaps, or what-have-you. I'd want to try the M4-style stock before plunking down any cash. It looks fairly low, meaning a proper cheek-weld may be hard to acquire. I bet Mossberg will sell a bunch of these rifles, though. They also have plenty of experience building twenty-twos. My first rifle was a bolt-action Mossberg, and they were everywhere when I was a kid. None of them had a threaded muzzle with a brake attached, which this latest SPX can be purchased with. Still, in its chest beats the lever-powered heart of a 19th century design. Mossberg also sells (or recently sold) a more conventional rifle.

A solution for the tactical cowboy? Mossberg's Model 464 SPX has lots of mounting points for lights or lasers, but runs like a traditional lever-action.

Winchester: This firm sold another solid rimfire lever-action rifle series known as the Model 9422. It was also available in .22 WMR. Too bad the Winchester rimfires have disappeared, since they were truly quality products. My old .22 LR XTR had nice wood with checkering, and shot extremely well. I wouldn't be afraid to snatch up a used one if it was priced right, but it probably will command high prices due to its growing collector value. For those who appreciate its lines, a Henry will make a close substitute.

SINGLE-SHOT RIFLES

As explained in the bolt-action section, many single-shot rifles are bolt-actions, minus a magazine system. Their virtue is simplicity, making them a popular introductory selection for younger shooters. Break-action barrel rifles are a completely different design. They are a simple system and most are reasonably priced. Thompson Center sells an economical and miniature .22 version of their famous Contender. Some, like the Rossi, are available as multi-barrel sets. A simple disassembly process permits an easy switch between rimfire, centerfire, and shotgun barrels. These rifles have potential for survival use. They offer utility at a reasonable price and can be disassembled for compact storage.

The break-action H&R Sportster is a simple and affordable time-tested design.

Rimfire falling-block rifles were very popular during the early 20th century. My grandfather's switch-barrel Stevens .32 rimfire is still in the family, but ammunition has long-since dried up. Savage reincarnated the .22 Favorite, but it's not listed on their 2013 website. On the high end of the spectrum, Winchester recently introduced a Model 1885 Low Wall chambered for their new .17 Winchester Super Mag rimfire cartridge. These rifles come out of the Miroku factory in Japan, which also built similar M1885s for Browning. Other recent chambering included .22 LR, .22 Magnum, .17 HMR, and .17 Mach 2. They're fantastic little falling blocks, but at around $1400, they aren't likely to see much planned survival use.

Oddballs: One example is the latest Savage .22/.410 selectable-barrel break-action gun. Even more unusual is Rossi's Circuit Judge convertible revolving rifle with interchangeable .22 LR and .22 WMR swing-out cylinders. It's different, to say the least. You'd likely need a zero change when switching between calibers. Both brands are really niche-type firearms, which may fill needs during true survival-based circumstances. I haven't used the Rossi, but I do have plenty of combination gun experience. Here's my take…

I wouldn't choose a combination gun as an end-all purchase. The concept seems initially sound, providing the best of both worlds with a rifle and shotgun all rolled into one package. In reality, what you'll quickly discover is that you own two single-shot firearms that require a bit of extra thinking to properly employ. As a combination gun freak, it pains me to admit this, and maybe with regular use, my ability would improve. Owning just this one type of gun should certainly improve the skills aspect, but other issues exist. Without an optical sight, any sort of precise or longer-range shooting will be difficult. Add one, and the intuitive pointing needed to make consistent shotgun hits on flying game will be lost. I've owned a European .223/12-gauge gun since 1980, and I still haven't figured out an ideal aiming system. It currently wears a small dot sight that somewhat compromises both barrels. The rifle barrel is underneath, which further complicates close-range aiming caused by bore and sight axis offset. It's still a handy tool at times, and I used it as recently as last week, but it fills an auxiliary role.

The Savage M-42 is a rimfire rifle and .410 shotgun rolled into one "combination gun" package.

The latest break-action Savage Model 42 Combination Gun is listed on their website under "specialty", which is a good call. It's a modernized version of their old Model 24 that was made for years in various calibers and gauges. I had a .22 LR/20-gauge version with a full choke barrel. I had it opened up to improved cylinder constriction to throw more open patterns. The rifle barrel was on top and was grooved for scope rings, but I stuck with iron sights. It saw some use on rabbits and spent time in the truck, seeing occasional use. Close range hits were easy, thanks to the close alignment of the rifle bore and low profile open sights. They didn't interfere with natural shotgun pointing, although the whole gun was a bit clunky. I really didn't hit many flying targets with it.

The new M-42 uses polymer for the stock and some other parts. It is listed in .22 LR/.410, with the rifle barrel still on top. A .22 WMR/.410 is also listed, and both versions can fire 3-inch Magnum .410 shells through the cylinder-bore barrel. No provision for optics exists, which is probably no big deal within the context of its practical limits. The .410 shotgun is a close-range proposition, no matter how you slice it. You aim the M-42 with built-in peep sights and switch barrels with a hammer-mounted selector lever. It looks harder to shoot at flying targets than my old M-24, but it is a whole lot lighter. A safety button is thrown in for good measure.

Although the M-42 (and similar guns) are not the ideal all-around choice for exploitation of a rimfire's full advantages, I could see having one stashed in a truck, aircraft, or some remote spot, reserved for true survival use. You could break it out and pop a rabbit or stationary spruce grouse to cook on a makeshift fire.

CHAPTER 5

CHOOSING A RIFLE

As we know by now, I'm into firearms that work the same. It simplifies and reinforces training to improve overall proficiency. In *Survival Guns: A Beginner's Guide*, a very basic four-gun system was shown. There were three that were shoulder-fired firearms, plus a handgun. The trio were all basic Remington pump guns: an M-870 shotgun, an M-557 .22 rimfire, and an M-7600 .308 centerfire rifle. Their safety buttons are all in the same spot, and these guns will run in all kinds of weather. Glamorous? Not so much. Legal just about everywhere? Yup. They're fairly affordable too, when priced as a three-gun system.

Well, maybe you're just not a pumpin' person. If not, life will continue and other choices exist. One thing that bothers me is a gun-rag article that poses a "which is better?" question, but doesn't deliver any sort of clear answer. We read it to learn the bottom line. When there isn't one, we feel jaded. So, after dragging you through the previous tortuous Chapter, I feel obligated to name a grand winner, along with a few other great picks.

THE TOP CHOICE

Up front, I'll say this one bugs me. My "systems" approach just got wobbly. The winner works just differently enough to undermine that principle but, weighing its many positive points against the very few negatives, the scale tips heavily in its favor. The top choice is a well-known semi-automatic.

Ruger's 10/22: Since it appeared in 1964, more than five million 10/22s have been produced. Ergonomics are right, as are its visual aspects. The Ruger just looks and feels like a real rifle. The rotary magazine is a brilliant design. The 10-shot version sits flush with the stock, but higher-capacity versions will interchange. It has been manufactured as a .22 WMR and .17 HMR, but neither is now available. If you buy a new one, it'll be a .22 LR version. Accuracy will be useful, if not spectacular.

As for mundane repairs, if Ruger packs up and moves to Albania, plenty of parts will be readily available for years to come. The rifle can be disassembled on a kitchen table with a screwdriver (for the stock) and pin punch. Barrel removal is a bit more complex, but only requires an Allen wrench. Keep it in factory-issue form and you won't need to go that far. You will want to remove the stock now and then, so the trigger group and bolt can be pulled out for cleaning.

Ruger 10/22 and all the tools needed for a basic field-strip.

Take reasonable care of a 10/22, and it should run for years. It's also reasonably priced and does its job as well. A standard version should suffice for many users. If not, a vast selection of aftermarket parts permits everything from modest tuning to a complete makeover. I'd resist the urge to go overboard, though. We want reliable function, decent accuracy and easy maintenance. Off the shelf, the Ruger will deliver. Add only those small parts necessary to meet any personalized needs and life will be good.

Those planning on extensive customization such as heavy barrels and tricked out stocks might consider a used 10/22. Go wild, and you can add an entire new trigger assembly, bolt, barrel, stock, and other doodads. There's a good chance the only remaining part will be the receiver, so a collection of unused factory parts will result.

The heart of this highly customized 10/22 is a Ruger receiver. Just about everything else is from Volquartsen.

Listing every possible option would result in dedicated Ruger 10/22 publication. Instead, let's look at some general categories:

Stocks: The basic 10/22 employs two mounting points. The main one is a screw located in the bottom of the forend, just ahead of the magazine. The other is a metal barrel band that encircles the forend tip and barrel. Loosening a small screw relieves enough tension to slip it forward and free of the stock. The bottom screw can then be loosened to free the action, which will lift out by elevating the muzzle end (the safety needs to be carefully centered first). Some other variants employ just the bottom screw. Probably the most popular aftermarket stock is the Hogue, which attaches in this manner. It can be had in various molded-in colors, as a hard or soft-textured "overmolded" version. Cost runs either side of $100, depending on its features. It's a comfortable and attractive upgrade that can be purchased with a standard small-diameter barrel channel, or a bull barrel cut. There are lots of other great picks as well, including some wild-looking laminated thumbhole types.

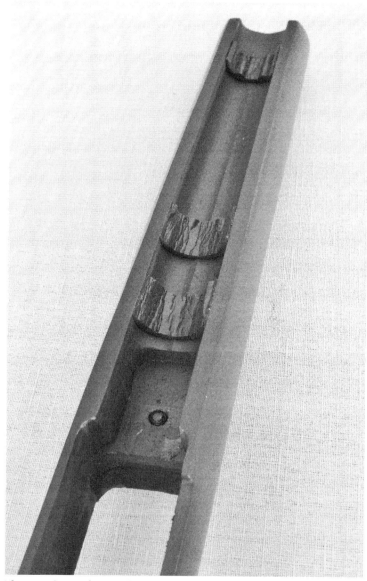

After-market 10/22 stock with bull-barrel channel. This one is retained with just one screw. A few strips of foam weather-stripping have been inserted to improve barrel harmonics.

Triggers: The standard 10/22 trigger is serviceable, but not spectacular. For rough use, that's not a bad thing. Still, an upgrade is an often sought feature. Drop-in parts or complete trigger assemblies can be purchased. The more expensive but safer bet is the latter, most of which cost somewhere around $200 or more. Volquartsen is well known for their excellent unit, but several others have appeared from firms like Timney or Kidd. With the stock dismounted, you simply drift out two pins for this conversion. Others may opt for replacement of just the factory innards, thereby saving some money. That's the route I took, using some Volquartsen parts. However, one new product worth a look is Ruger's BX-Trigger. It's a $90 upgrade that can easily be installed as a complete replacement unit, thereby solving a longstanding complaint of excessive pull weight by fussy shooters.

A factory-issue 10/22 trigger assembly. The hammer and safety are in a fired position.

Barrels: The factory barrel will actually cover just about all basic needs. It's also an irresistible candidate for customization due to the clever mounting system. With the barreled action removed from the stock, two cap screws will be exposed on the lower leading edge of the receiver. They cinch a horizontal clamping bar tightly into a dovetailed cut underneath the barrel, drawing it tightly rearward. A relieved barrel shank is first inserted into the receiver. Tightening the two cap screws then draws the barrel rearward until arrested by its shoulder. It's a strong and simple system. The standard factory barrel has a tapered sporter profile. Many of the aftermarket types use a thicker and heavier "bull barrel" profile that measures 0.920-inch. Each needs to be matched to a corresponding stock for proper fit. A huge amount of choices exist and some are quite expensive, running in excess of $350. Some innovative designs are used to satisfy those seeking a stiffer barrel without extra weight. Tactical Solutions has done well with their line of aluminum bull barrels, available in some interesting anodized colors. The actual barrel is a steel liner encased by an aluminum shroud. Volquartsen first popularized the concept with a carbon-fiber wrapped version. Many of the aftermarket barrels can be purchased with tricked-out compensators or threaded muzzles. Clark even sells a neat mid-weight barrel. Weight-saving flutes are often machined into barrels made from more conventional carbon or stainless steel materials. Some employ tighter "Bentz" chambers with minimal dimensions to maintain concentricity. They're also sometimes tight enough to interfere with extraction of a live round - something all such users should consider.

Ruger's barrel-mounting system with two rugged cap-screws. The clamping bar engages a dove-tail barrel cut, drawing it firmly into the receiver.

Bolts and small parts: Some die-hards actually switch out the entire factory bolt. It can be removed after separating the barreled action from the stock. The trigger group comes out next, along with a large bolt stop pin in the rear of the receiver. If you hold your mouth just right, you can work the bolt and recoil spring assembly free. Besides some fancy design work, the object of a custom bolt is minimal headspace (clearance between cartridge base and breech face) for more uniform ignition. Other 10/22 fans keep their factory bolts, but modify them. Firing pins are "pinned" to help control their travel. Aftermarket extractors provide a more secure

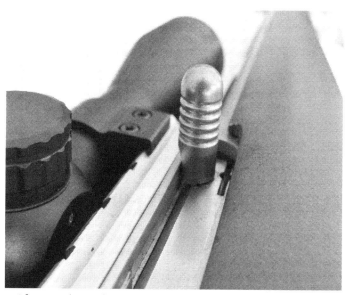

After-market Volquartsen tricked-out bolt handle assembly.

purchase to improve overall function. A trick bolt handle is part of the fun, whether needed or not. Among others, Volquartsen and Kidd enjoy good reputations.

Receivers: Those considering "the works" sometimes go with an entirely different receiver sold by Volquartsen, Tactical Solutions, Kidd, MOA, or several other firms. The material may be aluminum or steel, in carbon or stainless material. People in search of ultimate accuracy may choose one with a second, rear mounting point. The TS models actually employ a somewhat different, dual-recoil spring design, and can be had in the same eye-catching anodized colors as their barrels. Most customizers will use their Ruger receiver. One common addition is an extended magazine release. Unlike most other .22 rifles, the 10/22 lacks a grooved receiver. Instead, it's drilled and tapped. Due to the sheer numbers of rifles, plenty of scope bases are available. You can mount a combination Weaver slot/grooved base, Picatinny base, or what have you. Some of the custom receivers even include an integral base. A few have a rear port to accommodate a cleaning rod.

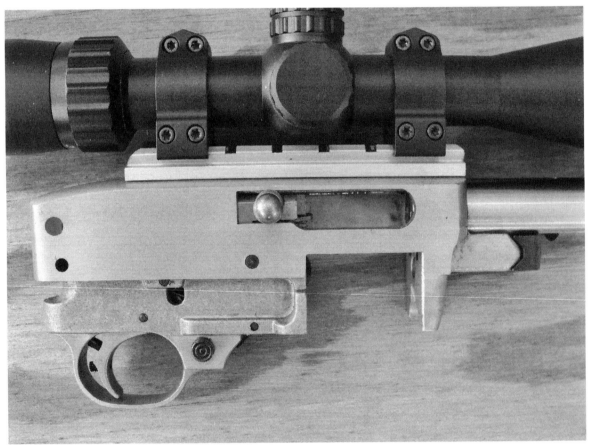

Factory Ruger 10/22 receiver with bolt locked rearward. Note the trigger-stop that limits extra motion during release.

Magazines: I much prefer the standard 10-shot factory versions, mainly because they seat flush. The higher-capacity 25-round (or greater) types certainly increase firepower, but they can also be a bother when slung with cold weather clothing. In fact, for the same reason and unlike most folks, I also can live with Ruger's older flush-mounted magazine release that is a bit bothersome. Ruger's latest clear plastic magazines seem like a nice way to ascertain remaining rounds (in good light). Regardless of your preference, they're all priced low enough to permit a good supply of extras.

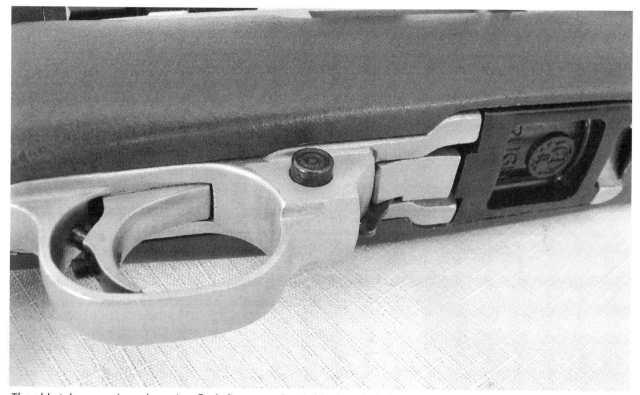

The old-style magazine release is a flush-fit rectangle, visible directly behind the magazine. Also shown is the adjacent bolt-release tab and safety button, which is on "safe".

<u>My own customized package:</u> It really just gradually evolved over a decade or more. I started with a bright finished, complete Ruger 10/22 receiver assembly that I was lucky enough to find. From there, I added a Brown Precision synthetic stock. The barrel was a Volquartsen stainless compensated .920 "sniper". I drilled and tapped the factory trigger to install a homemade overtravel stop. Later, a Volquartsen match sear and hammer were installed. The scope base is a one-piece Power Picatinny rail, just high enough to accept the extra bite of Warne QD scope rings. One set holds a 1" scope, and another set permits the fast exchange of a 30mm dot sight. I added an inexpensive ¼" cheek pad for a more comfortable gun mount. Since the whole thing happened over time, the cost was bearable. The biggest expense was the barrel, and the present one is actually its second. The initial VQ sniper shot everything great, except for a preferred target load. With several thousand rounds on hand, it was actually more cost-effective to sell the barrel and try another. The present VQ stainless, fluted, compensated HB tube looks pretty slick, and thankfully shoots everything well. Function has so far been 100%, and accuracy is near MOA. What do I have for my money? Well, mostly a tricked-out range rifle.

The author's evolutionary custom 10/22, set up for accuracy testing.

Again, such work is really unnecessary for basic survival-type requirements. In fact, some of it could get you in trouble. Dealing with a stuck live round in a dicey situation (probably involving low light) wouldn't be fun. Some of the aftermarket trigger modifications can produce an excellent pull, but function may be less positive. Add dirt, moisture, or cold weather, and it may not reset. As for "useful" accuracy, the factory barrel should be "minute of squirrel" grade. Expect it to shoot 2 MOA (or better), which translates to around an inch at fifty yards. Some do much better. A friend's circa-1982 Ruger Sporter shoots darned near as well as my custom 10/22. The only thing he did was send the trigger assembly to Clark for a $65 tune.

This Ruger 10-22 Deluxe Sporter will keep up with many highly customized versions. It's worth shooting some groups before tossing parts!

As of January 2015, the Ruger website lists six primary 10/22 models with individual variants. You can choose a small "Compact" rifle, a heavy-barreled "Target" version, or others. Weights run between 4 ½ to 7 ½ pounds. An even larger collection of "Distributor Exclusive" models is just this side of mind-numbing. They all run off the same great action, feeding from 10/22 magazines. Retail pricing starts below $300 and goes up towards $600, depending upon the features.

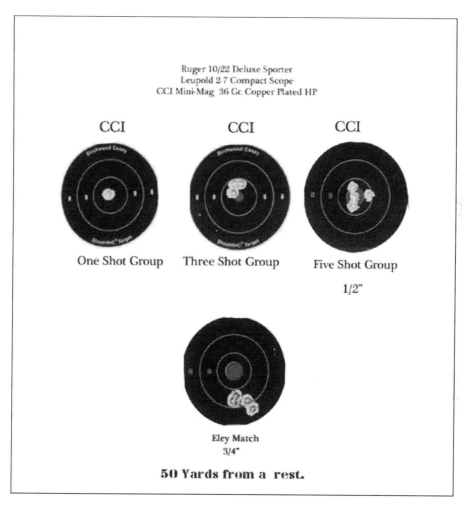

Great groups from a factory Ruger 10/22 barrel.

Ruger hasn't forgotten the ladies. Their pink 10/22 is a real eye-catcher.

The heavy-barreled 10/22 is another factory offering that also looks cool.

The latest takedown versions are in between, but seem especially well-suited for our needs. They maintain zero when reassembled, and will stow in a pack or vehicle. The stainless version makes a good, weather-resistant choice that comes with its own backpackable carrying case.

The Ruger 10/22 Take-down model is a strong candidate for survival use. It reassembles in seconds without losing zero.

Another really strong contender is Ruger's 2014, 50th Anniversary Model. Besides a stainless barrel, you get the latest modular synthetic stock design, which was introduced with Ruger's innovative American rimfire bolt-action series (more on that shortly). A combination peep sight/Picatinny scope base is already mounted to the receiver. The muzzle end sports a rugged-looking front sight and a threaded muzzle with a flash hider attached. The whole thing weighs only around 5 pounds, and retail cost is $379 (as of late 2014). It disappeared from the 2015 listings, but should still exist in the supply line. If not, you could build your own facsimile, thanks to the abundance of aftermarket parts.

One of the neatest-looking 10/22s I've seen was a very basic shooter conversion. While perusing the tables at a gun show, an attractive Ruger backed me up. Come to find out it was just a plain blued 10/22 carbine in a black Hogue synthetic stock. It was simple, but very attractive. Add that Ruger BX trigger assembly and you'd have a downright useful rifle, which could be customized in stages. In fact, Hogue has just announced that a stock for the Takedown Ruger is forthcoming.

I wish the 10/22 had a last-shot lockback feature. I wish it had the means to accept a breech-inserted cleaning rod. It doesn't, and although both issues can be addressed, neither is probably worth the bother. But even in its basic form, the Ruger 10/22 is not only the top semi-auto pick, but also the first place rimfire rifle winner.

OTHER SEMI-AUTO CHOICES

While we're into semi-autos, a runner-up seems advisable. We have one, based on sheer numbers, price, and dependability.

Marlin's Model 60: A basic M-60 with a 14-shot tubular magazine and plain wood stock is inexpensive. The detachable-magazine, synthetic stocked Model 795 variant is often advertised for even less. Slightly more costly versions are offered in different finishes with camo stocks, or stainless steel and laminated construction. Both the M-60 and M-795 will lock open on their last shot, and run reliably with only occasional maintenance. Read the manual, and you should be able to disassemble either without undue difficulty. The receivers are grooved for easy scope mounting, and sling swivel studs are standard on some variants.

Marlin's basic model 60 is not only affordable but accurate. The last shot lock-back feature is a nice touch.

I really like my M-60SS, which has a laminated stock and stainless metal. Besides looking sharp, it handles well and has a couple extra features, including sling studs, a folding rear sight, and a high visibility orange front sight. Some folks will like that color, but I switched mine out for a fiber-optic front blade. I always keep a full "Spee-D-Loader" on hand to load its 14-shot magazine.

The Model 795SS is similarly furnished, but has a synthetic stock. M-795 owners should pick up extra magazines available as either 7 or 10-shot versions. If memory serves me right, mine came with a 7-shot type, but Marlin now lists M-795s with 10-round capacity.

The Model 70PSS takedown variant should have greater appeal to some. Unscrew a knurled retaining nut, and the barrel will detach for compact travel in a floating case. It's a well-appointed and very compact package, listed at only 3 ¼ pounds! The detachable magazine holds 7-shots but will interchange with standard 10-round types.

While the Ruger 10/22 seems to draw more attention, Marlin maintains an affordable line of handy .22 rifles.

Remington's Model 597: Although this rifle is relatively "new", it does have a track record spanning nearly two decades. Like the Marlins, it also locks open on the last shot. The 10-round .22 LR magazine sits flush and the current synthetic-stock rifles are fairly lightweight. Several types are sold, including a short 16-inch heavy-barreled variant without sights in several stock colors, a lighter contoured 20-inch version with a threaded muzzle; and a 20-inch sporter with open sights. You can even buy camo-stocked models in some wild patterns like "Muddy Girl".

The option to mount a scope with either the grooved receiver or a Weaver-type base will be appreciated by some shooters. The iron sighted model could benefit from a set of QD rings on a Weaver-type one-piece base.

A .22 WMR Remington M-597 in basic form, with a Nikon scope.

A 100-yard .22 WMR group fired from a laminated Model 597.

Of interest to some semi-auto fans will be the availability of the same 20-inch configuration chambered for .22 WMR. Some will spring for both calibers. The M-597 isn't as modular as a Ruger 10/22, but Volquartsen does sell an aftermarket trigger and hammer. New rifles are affordable, and older ones can often be found in the "used" racks of gun shops. Some of the previous laminated stock rifles are pretty sharp, although noticeably heavier. Supposedly, the earliest M-597s had some magazine problems. Newer rifles run better and extra magazines are available. One variant to avoid is the .17 HMR. It had lots of problems, and is unsafe to shoot.

S&W's M&P 15-22: I wouldn't buy this rimfire AR-15 carbine knock-off unless it was intended to compliment a centerfire AR-15. The Ruger or Marlin will do the same thing in a more conventional configuration that places your eye closer to the bore, for less money. For survival purposes, hits on edible targets will thus be easier to accomplish at various ranges, especially those inside 10 yards. Not that a .22 configured as an AR-15 won't work; it will, with practice.

Those with .22 LR M-597 reliability issues should try the latest 3rd-generation magazines.

S&W's 15-22 with two magazine options. The shorter 10-shot satisfies some local requirements, and works better off a bench. The hi-cap version holds 25 rounds of .22 LR..

Easy maintenance due to no gas system. The S&W .22 is a simple blow-back design.

But, in deference to the many folks who will wind up with a centerfire AR-15, the .22 version does make sense. The S&W .22 runs like the real deal and is actually easier to maintain. In areas that limit magazine capacity, the 10-shot version should put you in the game. Smith & Wesson's MOE model provides most of the features you may want in a 5.56 carbine. With planning, you could field a useful pair of firearms, using the rimfire as a neat little trainer. The S&W .22 does have a couple of other interesting attributes. The versions with A-2 flash hiders have standard 1/2x28-pattern muzzle threads that will accept suppressors (after following BATF regulations). Also, the upper and lower receiver halves can be easily separated by manually pulling two pins. The result is a very lightweight package that won't occupy much space.

Manual depression of two pins separates the lower and upper receivers for compact storage..

The Henry U.S. Survival AR-7: This choice is presented for those seeking a last ditch rifle of absolute minimal size and weight. Once disassembled, it will fit in nearly any bug-out kit. The pair of 8-shot magazines provide reasonable amount of .22 LR fire-power. It's a fairly weather-resistant rifle that can be assembled quickly without tools. The list-price of under $350 makes it a possible spare gun contender.

SEMI-AUTO RIMFIRE SAMPLER: Prices shown are approximate retail, effective 2015						
Rifle	**Magazine**	**bbl**	**.22 LR**	**.22 WMR**	**.17 HMR**	**Price**
Browning	TM 12 rd	19.25"	Yes	–	–	$625
CZ M-512	DM 5 rd	20.60"	Yes	Yes	–	$480+

Rifle	Magazine	bbl	.22 LR	.22 WMR	.17 HMR	Price
Henry AR-7 Surv	DM 8 rd	16.50″	Yes	—	—	$270
Mag Research	DM 10 & 9	17″	Yes	Yes	Yes	$700+
Marlin M-60	TM 14 rd	19″	Yes	—	—	$250
Marlin M-795	DM 10 rd	18″	Yes	—	—	$200
Rem M-552	TM 20-15	21″	S-L-LR	—	—	$540
Rem M-597	DM 10 & 8	20″	Yes	Yes	—	$250+
Ruger 10/22	DM 10 rd	18.50″	Yes	—	—	$260+
Savage M-64FSS	DM 10 rd	20.25″	Yes	—	—	$260
S&W M&P 15-22	DM 10 & 25	16″	Yes	—	—	$450+

Representative models: Other configurations & bbl lengths available.   DM: Detachable Magazine TM: Tubular Magazine

Not every person will want a semi-auto, and sometimes preference just depends on what we grow up with. In many parts of rural America, people still tote lever-actions. Others carry pumps. Bolt-actions are probably more widely used than either. If those preferences involve big game rifles, a similar .22 makes lots of sense. To that end, a few popular rimfire examples are included here. And of course, once again, it's not easy to nail one "best" choice.

LEVER-ACTION PICKS

With either of these choices, you'll gain an ambidextrous system having much in common with a centerfire relative. The Marlin should keep traditionalists happy. The Browning will match up with their BLR series that fires modern centerfire calibers.

Marlin's Model 39A lever-action: So many centerfire rifles exist that we can't ignore this system. Many are bound to be pressed into service if things go belly up, and believe it or not, their owners will be suitably armed. Odds are good that the big-bore rifles will be either Winchesters or Marlins. Both make a good choice, but only the Marlin survives as originally offered. The high-quality Winchester Model 9422 has unfortunately faded away.

Happily, the Marlin .22 lives on. It eats Shorts, Longs, or Long Rifle ammo, and it takes down, too. Turn a large knurled knob on the receiver's right side, and you'll have a two-piece rifle. Plenty of used Marlins are out there, just begging for a good home. With so much attention focused on black rifles, the possibility of a good deal still exists. Unlike the Ruger 10/22, you can clean a Model 39 from the breech. Basic field stripping is fairly straightforward. With blued steel and a walnut stock, you get a good solid rifle for a fair price. It will feel right in your hands, and shoot well, too. Pair one up with a .30/30 for a useful set of rifles. Any revolver shooters could also add a .357 Magnum Marlin. All will look and operate similarly for both right and left-handed shooters.

A pair of practical receiver-sight Marlins in rimfire and centerfire versions.

Browning's BL-22 lever-action: Here's another solidly-built rifle that would also compliment an excellent Browning centerfire BLR. Both share a unique rack and pinion action with a shorter, 33-degree lever throw. The centerfire model feeds from a detachable box magazine, permitting use of modern calibers with pointed bullets. The rimfire uses a tubular magazine that will digest three .22 caliber flavors. Other than that they're pretty similar. Several BL-22 grades are offered, including some with engraving. Any BL-22 is a very handsome rifle and one that carries well. Mine shot accurately enough to cover most bases. For any BLR users, the BL-22 is a must-have addition. A three-gun set in .22 LR, .223, and .308 would cover just about anything. You can even buy a takedown high-power BLR!

LEVER-ACTION RIMFIRE SAMPLER: Prices shown are approximate retail, effective 2015						
Rifle	**Magazine**	**bbl**	**.22 LR**	**.22 WMR**	**.17 HMR**	**Price**
Browning BL Series	TM 22-15	20″	S-L-LR	—	—	$520
Henry Classic	TM 21-11	20″	S-L-LR	Yes	Yes	$300+
Marlin M39	TM 26-19	24″	S-L-LR	—	—	$565
Mossberg M464 SPX	TM 14 rd	18″	Yes	—	—	$500
Representative models: Other configurations & bbl lengths available. *TM: Tubular Magazine.*						

PUMP GUN CHOICE

This one is easy. It matches nicely with the practical Remington shotgun and rifle choices shown in *Survival Guns: A Beginner's Guide:*

Remington's Model 572 Fieldmaster: This .22 rifle makes the short list primarily because of its affiliation with the all-star Remington Model 870 shotgun and Model 7600 rifle. All share a common pump-action and standard fire control locations. The M572's iron sights match those on an 870 slug barrel and Model 7600 rifle.

Like many other .22s, the Fieldmaster's steel receiver is grooved for scope rings. Its tubular magazine will handle .22 Shorts, Longs or Long Rifles. Slip in some Shorts or CB Caps and you gain "Magnum" airgun-type performance for extremely quiet shooting. The M572 is a bit of a bother to thoroughly clean, but then again, being a manually cycled pump, you shouldn't have to do that too often.

For those who like pumps, the Remington remains a logical choice. It's no Cadillac, but it does the job, and actually, the latest BDL version really won't hurt your eyes. Again, when matched up with a Remington centerfire Model 7600 .308 pump rifle, one can gain a very relevant trainer. Add a 12-gauge pump, and you're ready for just about anything!

A new M572 is actually fairly pricey, but because it has been around in one form or another for decades, used rifles can also be found for fairly reasonable cost.

SLIDE-ACTION RIMFIRE SAMPLER: Prices shown are approximate retail, effective 2015						
Rifle	Magazine	bbl	.22 LR	.22 WMR	.17 HMR	Price
Rem M572 BDL	TM 20-15	21"	S-L-LR	–	–	$550
Henry Octagon	TM 21-12 rd	19.5"	S-L-LR	Yes	–	$500
Representative models: Other configurations & bbl lengths available. TM: Tubular Magazine						

BOLT-ACTIONS

The next edition in our book series will deal with centerfire rifles. Bolt-actions will be among them, and Remington's Model 700 will play a dominant (but not exclusive) role. With an eye towards common function, choose your weapon…

Marlin or Savage: Balancing features and performance against cost, either brand is hard to beat. Both share functional similarity with the tried and true Remington 700 centerfire, and the safety buttons are all in the same location. Marlin and Savage offer a large array of rimfire versions with wood or synthetic stocks and blued or stainless actions. The latest trigger designs provide great let-offs, too. Models are available in .22 LR, .22 WMR, and .17 HMR.

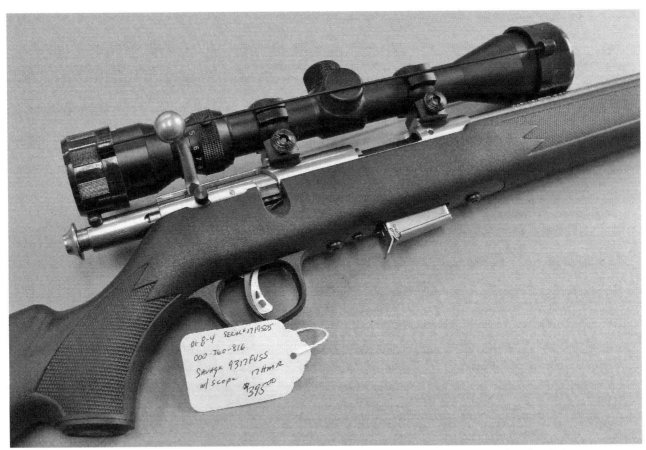

An inexpensive but race-ready .17 HMR Savage M-9317 Package Gun, factory-equipped with a 3x9 scope.

Savage still sells a .17 Mach 2 as well. They also produce interesting short-barreled rifles with threaded muzzles and, going to the other extreme, small-bore "tactical" offerings. Speaking of "extreme", their thumbhole stock/spiral-fluted model is a guaranteed attention-grabber. By all accounts, it shoots very well. As I've found out the hard way, it's possible to spend a lot more money on a rifle that won't be as accurate.

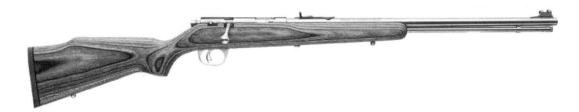

Marlin Model XT MTSL with a laminated stock and loss-free tubular magazine.

Marlin offers tubular-magazine models and both companies include sling swivel studs – seemingly minor but very handy additions. Package rifles come complete with pre-mounted, bore-sighted scopes. I really like the laminated stocks for a couple of reasons. First, they're quieter than synthetics, and secondly, the trigger guards aren't molded in. Both are admittedly minor points, but it's nice to be able to replace a broken guard. I prefer the clip-fed rifles, but then again, a tubular magazine won't disappear in the woods or snow.

Juniors won't be excluded, and any left-handed shooters can choose a Savage.

Ruger Model 77 Rimfires: For any fans of Ruger's Model 77 centerfire rifles, their rimfire line is really worth a look. All use rotary magazines, which differ from the 10/22 type, but work equally well.

The actions are bank vault tough and machined for Ruger's rugged proprietary scope rings. Rifles are available in blued or stainless steel with wood, synthetic or laminated stocks. All three mainstream rimfire calibers are offered, and those I've shot performed very well.

Cost is nearly double what you'll spend for a Marlin or Savage, running more to centerfire prices. Still, those looking for a tough and handsome, well-laid-out rifle may wish to look at the Rugers. Their centerfire Model 77 rifles remain popular, so the rimfires are a logical extension of that system.

Ruger's laminated Model 77 rimfire. This one's a .17 HMR.

I'll be curious to see if this line continues in light of the new Ruger "American", which retails for half the cost.

Ruger American? Here's a way to get back on system-based ground at the risk of an unproven design. But in this case, the overall concept, which is offered by a well-established manufacturer, seems excellent. I'm betting the newest Ruger .22 will really sell. It seems well-conceived, particularly in regard to the scope mounting systems, which really do cover all bases (literally). Like its new centerfire twin, the .22 version has a tang-mounted safety. The bedding system looks great, so with a good barrel, accuracy should follow. The bolt release is another fine feature, as is the adjustable trigger. Useful iron sights are standard, and the interchangeable length-of-pull and comb pieces are brilliant. Unscrewing the rear sling stud permits their exchange, and extra units sell for only $20.

The American's 10/22 magazine compatibility is just the icing on the cake. The $329 retail sticker will get you into either a short or full-size version. The .22 WMR chambering will be appreciated, and a .17 HMR has followed. The hardest part might involve choosing between the carbine model and a full-size version. Again, the use of abundant 10/22 magazines is a strong selling point. This rimfire would perfectly compliment Ruger's centerfire American series, which is also available in short or full-size models. It would also make a great addition to a Ruger 10/22.

BOLT-ACTION RIMFIRE SAMPLER: Prices shown are approximate retail, effective 2015						
Rifle	Magazine	bbl	.22 LR	.22 WMR	.17 HMR	Price
Browning T-Bolt	DM 10 rd	22″	Yes	Yes	Yes	$650
CZ American 455	DM 5 rd	20.5″	Yes	Yes	Yes	$425+
Marlin XT	DM 7 rd	22″	Yes	Yes	Yes	$250+
Marlin XT T	TM 25-12	22″	S-L-LR	Yes	Yes	$250+
Ruger American	DM 10-9	22″	Yes	Yes	Yes	$330+
Ruger M77	DM 10-9	20″	Yes	Yes	Yes	$650
Savage M93SS	DM 4 rd	21″	Yes	Yes	Yes	$280
Savage Rascal (youth)	Single-shot	16″	Yes	—	—	$160
Representative models: Other configurations & bbl lengths available. DM: Detachable Magazine TM: Tubular Magazine						

COMBINATION GUNS

They do occupy a niche, and many have no doubt been sold to survival-minded people. These guns are popular in Europe and most are fairly expensive. For our purposes, a utilitarian combo gun will do. It's one of those things that could conceivably be stashed somewhere for emergency use.

Savage Model 42: The latest Savage combo gun has no long-term history, but it is compact and lightweight due to polymer components. It won't accept a scope but it's really not that kind of gun, anyway. The presence of one in a remote setting would be as reassuring as a cooking fire.

COMBINATION GUN SAMPLER: Prices shown are approximate retail, effective 2015						
Rifle	Chamber	bbl	.22 LR	.22 WMR	.17 HMR	Price
Savage M42	3″ .410 plus ->	20″	Yes	Yes	—	$370

Common .22 Shorts or CB Caps would emit almost no noise. The .22 WMR version would provide some extra punch.

CHAPTER 6

SIGHTING SYSTEM BASICS

A decent optical sighting system is beneficial, especially on a rifle capable of decent accuracy. Useful range can be increased, and precise shot placement will be possible on tiny targets. The most common optical system is telescopic sight, more widely known as a "scope". Electronic dot sights are another popular choice. Unlike scopes, they normally don't provide magnification, but instead display a small electronic dot for quick target acquisition. Basic iron sights still have a place as well.

Of course, optics can fail. My serious shootin' irons are equipped with quick-disconnect mounts *and* backup iron sights. You never really know when things will go south, so it's reassuring to have a backup plan. Many moons ago on an out-of-state hunt, a pants leg fetched up on a barbed wire strand while crossing an old stone wall after dark. Things happened fast and I had a serious list to starboard on the way back to the truck. Its headlights revealed a nasty ding on the scope, and the following morning was lost just trying to sort things out. Sure enough, the rifle was hopelessly out of zero, as determined by two sighting shots. Attempts to re-zero it turned out to be futile, so the next headache involved locating tools to remove its scope rings. Luckily, the rifle had iron sights that I'd taken the time to adjust. Those of us who hunt recognize the best hours normally occur at dawn and dusk. My iron sights, which worked well enough on a range in full daylight, turned out to be pretty much useless during prime time. They were better than nothing, but the overall situation was compromised. Things went downhill from there, but I did learn a few lessons.

During another trip, years later and two thousand miles from home, a guide ran over my rifle. It was in a hardshell case, which is now shaped differently. Its contents somehow managed to survive except for a scope sunshade, which is an elliptical reminder of Murphy's Law. This time, I had a spare rifle and the hunt continued, producing positive results.

With a rimfire rifle, things may be a tad less serious. We'll probably be somewhere close to home, pursuing small game or cans. I don't feel obligated to have QD scope rings or iron sights, although they can prove useful.

IRON SIGHTS

There are two kinds of iron sight users: those who have trouble seeing them; and those who will. The older we become the harder iron sights will be to use. I've found fiber-optic front sights help. A light-gathering front sight element tends to really stand out, permitting better resolution during most conditions. Being partially color blind I have a hard time seeing red. Green works for me and I choose a diameter suited to a firearm's anticipated use. Big game rifles may benefit from a large insert, which *really* stands out in low light. For small game a finer element helps.

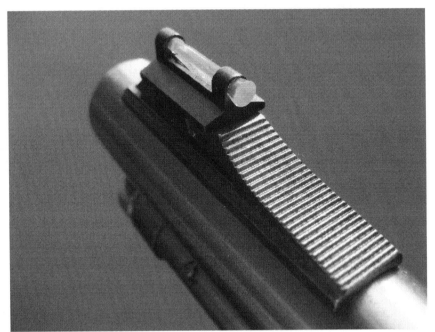

This fiber-optic Hi-Viz front sight has interchangeable elements. It really stands out in low light.

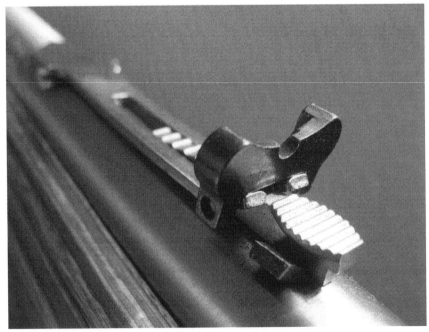

A rear sight with a stepped elevator. This one folds down for scope clearance.

Open sights: The most common types of iron sights are often referred to as "open sights". They are often factory supplied with .22 rifles, especially on plinker-type guns. Open sights consist of two components: a front bead and a notched rear blade. When both are properly aligned on a target, hits should result, assuming they are properly indexed to the firearm. Many rear sights have a stepped elevator for vertical adjustments. Windage (left and right) is typically adjusted by drifting the rear sight in its mounting dovetail (always move the REAR sight in the direction you want your bullets to go). Open sights have been around for centuries and they still have a place. Nothing could be simpler, more weatherproof, or quicker to use. For close-range shooting, they'll do, but at longer range, particularly on small targets, things can get challenging. In low light, the traditional designs can be extremely hard to see. Ideally, the shooter should focus on the front sight. For my old eyes, that highly visible fiber-optic insert makes this possible.

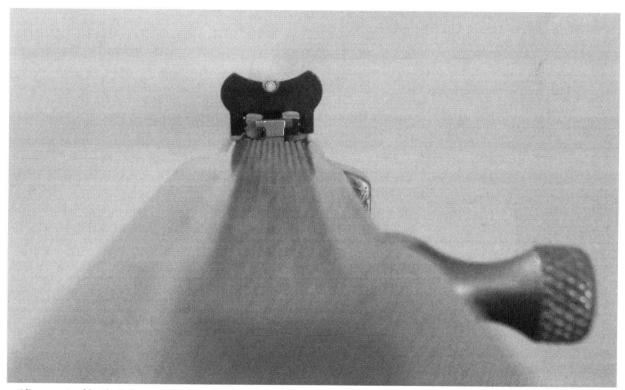

Alignment of both sights results in a "sight picture". Once adjusted so bullets impact on top of the front sight, the rifle is "sighted in".

Peep sights: Adding a peep (or aperture) rear sight can improve accuracy. The most expensive small-bore match rifles have precision sights, which cost more than many .22 rifles. They permit great accuracy, but useful field results can be achieved with the more basic types. Our eyes will naturally center an object in a hole, so aligning a front sight in a properly-sized rear aperture can support consistent shooting. The rear doesn't need to be as small as one might imagine, either. The shooter just looks through the hole, focusing on the front sight without conscious alignment. The right combination can actually be pretty fast and intuitive.

A collection of "peep" or aperture rear sights. The one on the left is a Lyman, mounted on a Marlin M-39 lever-action .22 rifle.

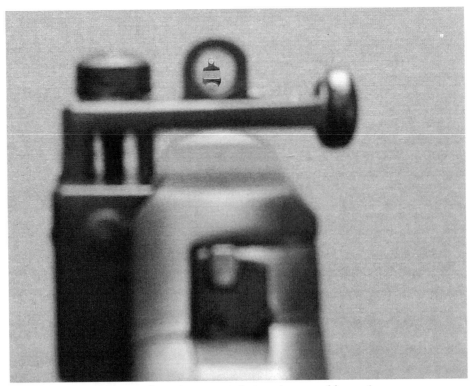

The large ghost-ring peep is fast and reasonably precise.

Iron and peep sight examples: I have two Marlin .22s with aftermarket green fiber-optic front sights. An open-sighted semi-automatic Marlin Model 60 .22 is a blast for close-range work on moving targets. The highly visible bead is easy to pick up, and works well on tossed cans. It's strictly a fast-paced plinking rifle.

A second Model 39 lever-action .22 has a receiver-mounted Lyman peep sight equipped with a "ghost ring" aperture. The threaded sighting disk has been removed, and its large housing becomes the surrogate peep. Logic would dictate loss of precision, but the huge rear aperture actually works. The green fiber-optic front bead is a visual grabber, and my eye automatically centers it. Low light performance greatly improves, and shot groups will be better than one might expect. I had a Marlin .45/70 big-bore identically equipped. The front sight employed a larger "Hi-Viz" element for use on big game in thick, dark spruce. It was an effective and weatherproof tool.

Because I work on a range, lunchtime entertainment sometimes involves a bit of recreational trick-shooting. Targets could be edgewise playing cards, standing .22 casings, head-on 9mm brass, or even houseflies, most of which will be within 10 paces. Such pinpoint shooting is actually easier with the sights as close to the barrel as possible, and either of these iron sighted rifles fills that bill. I recently saw a well-known shooter attempt similar shots with a .22 AR-15. It was painful to watch. The rifle was obviously sighted for a greater distance. At close range, the extreme sight height relative to the bore meant that targets needed to be covered up to be hit. Aiming "guesstimation" was necessary, which didn't work very well at all. The same problem can happen afield when trying to fill a camp pot. More than one ruffed grouse has been blown to smithereens by a low hit intended for its noggin.

SCOPES

Increased distances, smaller targets, and older eyes are a recipe for optics. Most of the comments here are applicable to all scopes, whether intended for centerfire *or* rimfire rifles. However, airguns introduce a concern related to their recoil. Believe it or not, you can unravel a quality firearm scope in short order if it isn't built to withstand the snappy reverse jolt of a spring-powered rifle!

What the numbers mean: We'll often see scopes cataloged with numbers like "3-9x40mm". The 3-9 indicates its magnification range, and the 40mm is the diameter of the forward (objective) lens in millimeters. In this case, the scope would be a widely used "variable power" design, providing a telescopic image range of from three to nine magnifications. Another model might be advertised as a 4x32, which would more than likely be a fixed four-power type with a 32mm objective. Binoculars are listed similarly, a 10x40 being a popular choice. Magnification isn't everything, and too much can introduce problems. Once understood, the relationship of these numbers will help us make a practical choice.

Most dot sights don't employ magnification and use a relatively large-diameter tube for fast aiming. The dot will be listed in "MOA" terms, indicating its relative size to a target. It will still use lenses to reflect and display an illuminated aiming point. We'll take a closer look at these units in the next section.

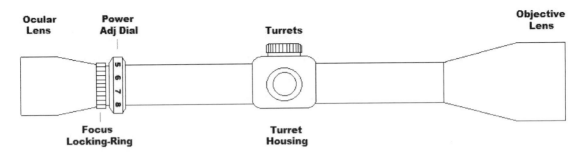

Ocular Lens | Power Adj Dial | Turrets | Objective Lens

Focus Locking-Ring | Turret Housing

Basic scope nomenclature. This one is a variable-power with adjustable magnification. The ocular lens is adjustable for individual eyes. The turrets provide adjustments to sight it in.

Basic scope design: A telescopic sight is a metal tube that houses a series of lenses and some sort of internal aiming point. The latter is often a pair of bisecting "crosshairs" that are aligned with a target. This system is known as a "reticle", and it is housed within a smaller, moveable internal tube. Opposing external knobs on the scope's main body contact the interior reticle housing so the rifle can be "zeroed". At that point, bullets should strike a spot indicated by alignment of the reticle and target. Each knob typically works with graduated click-stops to precisely control reticle movement.

The whole process sounds fairly simple, and it is, assuming quality is factored in. Most of today's scopes are manufactured with aluminum main tubes, which are externally similar. However, the innards may be quite different, explaining the wide variety of costs. Consistent adjustments require tight tolerances and durable materials. A variable scope will also have extra moving parts connected to a power selector ring. Cheaper scopes will sometimes have plastic internal lenses, as well as clickers made from the same substances. Internal components will be more lightly engineered to help keep pricing low.

A decent scope will have good glass throughout, secured in close tolerance supports. Moveable parts will interface on durable surfaces, and the culmination of optical quality and construction will ensure consistent accuracy. The scope and its internals will become a body at rest during recoil, so its parts will be braced to withstand this force. Spring-powered piston airguns recoil in the opposite direction and produce considerable vibration. Unless an airgun-rated scope is purchased, it may not survive for long. We cover this in *Air Rifles: A Buyer's and Shooter's Guide*, but it's worth noting right now.

These Burris field-type elevation and windage turrets have their caps removed for adjustments. Not the click-values indicated inside the elevation cap.

A big factor for all shooters is light transmission. A small portion of light is lost during its passage through each lens, and special coatings can help reduce this problem. Their application, along with anti-reflective internal tube measures and good lenses, will result in a nice bright image. The scope can then be atmospherically purged and filled with an inert gas like nitrogen to prevent fogging.

Brightness: A large-diameter scope tube or objective lens is no guarantee of brightness. Good low-light performance requires quality construction and a few other factors. Among them is the "exit pupil". If you point the front end of a scope at a bright lamp, a shaft of light will be emitted from its rear. By holding a piece of blank paper 3-5" away, you can note the spot where full diameter occurs. That's your "exit pupil", which contains the actual image your eye will see. You can calculate the diameter by dividing a scope's objective by its magnification. A 10x40mm scope will magnify you target ten times and have a front lens 40mm in diameter. It will also produce a 4mm exit pupil.

However, the human eye has limits. Our pupils will dilate in low light, but most won't open beyond 7mm. increasing the objective lens of the same 10X scope to 50mm will result in a larger exit pupil, emitting an image roughly 5mm in diameter. You'll have a "brighter" scope, but one not quite sufficient for full advantage at dusk or dawn. The scope will also be much larger, and possibly hard to mount. A more practical solution would be less magnification. A well-built 40mm 3x9 will emit an 8mm exit pupil on 5-power, and do a better job. The operative phrase here is "well-built".

Cost: Perhaps in ignorance, many folks who would spend good money on a high-powered rifle optic will spend no more than the absolute minimum on a .22 rifle. I just priced a useful Marlin Model XT 22 stainless bolt-action, which ran slightly below $300. It would be a good, accurate, weatherproof, and fairly affordable rifle, capable of fulfilling all reasonable requirements. It's worthy of more than a thirty dollar scope! I'm NOT saying you need to spend another $300 for glass, but you might be wise to consider something in between. The proliferation of optics, combined with more efficient manufacturing, has resulted in usable scopes for a fair price. For another $150 (tops), you could assemble a package capable of hitting quarters from a solid rest at 50 paces. Once you got off those sandbags, you could work on field position practice to really improve your ability.

Parallax: One potential problem for rimfire and airgun shooters involves a condition whereby the image and the crosshairs diverge. The resulting internal misalignment can cause shot group shifts without perfectly centered eye placement. The reticle (crosshairs) and image will only coincide at one distance, so most centerfire scopes are parallax corrected for 100 or 150 yards. If you aim at a close target, don't be surprised to see the crosshairs wander as your head

An adjustable-objective (AO) feature permits fairly precise parallax adjustments (PA), which improves accuracy at both ends of the range spectrum. The numbers indicate yardage.

shifts position. This effect can be especially pronounced at short rimfire and airgun ranges. The reticle and target will be on different planes, and you'll be experiencing parallax.

High magnification varmint or target scopes often have a parallax adjustment (PA) feature, which permits range corrections calibrated to a yardage scale. Many employ a rotating front bell (objective lens), which is twisted until a small witness mark on the scope's tube coincides with the appropriate distance setting. Lately, side-mounted parallax adjustment models have become popular. The PA knob is located on the turret housing, opposite the windage dial. Fine tuning is thus more convenient, especially from prone. Regardless of the design, in theory the graduations will reflect the actual yardage to eliminate parallax. Unfortunately, this is not always the case, especially with lower-priced scopes. While many are built for long range shooting, others are designed specifically for very close rimfire and airgun targets. Some manufacturers market lower-cost rimfire PA models to entice spend-thrift shooters.

You'll really need a purpose-built rimfire scope for best results at closer ranges. It will either offer close-range PA dialing, or be permanently parallax corrected for around 50 yards. Either system will do. The PA scopes offer more precision, but are generally larger and more expensive. The simpler, internally corrected models are built for hunting and tend to be smaller, lower magnification scopes. They're cheaper to build and a safer bet for budget conscious shooters.

Size: With careful shopping, you can sometimes combine the PA feature with more compact dimensions. I really don't like an oversized scope on a graceful rifle. Balance is thrown out of whack and the combination just looks weird. Most U.S. scopes have a one-inch diameter main tube, although inexpensive rimfire units are still sold with 7/8" diameters. The latest trend involves a proliferation of European 30mm (or 1.2") scope tubes, combined with high magnification. Some folks think the bigger tubes gather more light, but their main purpose is to provide more interior room for increased elevation adjustments, electronics, or both. Most of these scopes are *really* big! The 7/8-inch models are *really* cheap! For rimfire use, a 1" tube is a good compromise, providing adequate strength, sufficient adjustments, and a wide selection of mounting options.

Anschutz M-1516 heavy-barreled .22 LR with Burris 4x12 AO. It makes a great centerfire trainer, but it's a bit large for general-purpose use..

The largest rimfire scope I own is on a heavy-barreled .22 Anschutz bolt gun. It's a 1" Burris 4-12 adjustable objective (AO) Rimfire/Airgun Scope. The overall package is fairly hefty and geared towards precise, scaled-down centerfire training. It's not my first choice for a small game safari. The scope's parallax scale goes down to 7 yards, which is closer than I'll ever use. I normally park it at 50 yards, but often dial it to other ranges as circumstances dictate. Eye relief is a bit touchy at the highest magnification settings, which is why they are reserved for bench rest work. Below 10X, things seem right, and 8X is more than enough for most shooting. The rifle and scope make a good match for their intended use, but a general purpose .22 will benefit from a smaller scope, avoiding excess weight and top-heavy handling.

Magnification: My sporter-weight .22 LR Remington Model 504 bolt-action has a correspondingly smaller 3-9 Burris with a parallax-adjustable objective lens. It looks just right and handles well. The power ring usually stays on 5X, which is all I normally need afield. Taking things down another notch, my older and smaller Remington M-510 single-shot bolt rifle wears an inexpensive 4X Bushnell rimfire scope, factory-adjusted for 50 yards. It too is well-proportioned, and the lower magnification hasn't been a hindrance for its utilitarian role. A 2-7 is another great pick, and a 3x9 is more than enough glass. Those popping prairie dogs with a .17 HMR might opt for a 4-12 on a super-accurate varminter.

People with variable-power scopes should shoot groups on several power settings. You may see noticeable group shifts! I always test for this by shooting 5-shot groups from 50 yards at 3X, 6X, and 9X. The cheaper scopes are more likely to cause problems due to tolerance slop. If you run into this situation, a simple fix is to choose an all-around magnification setting (like 5X) and leave the power ring alone. The best insurance against this phenomenon is a quality scope.

Field of view (FOV): As magnification increases, the field of view decreases. This is the horizontal area that can be viewed through the scope, and is normally expressed as a measurement in feet at 100 yards. A 3-9 scope might have a 32-foot FOV on its lowest setting, but only 12 feet on full power. Close-range targets will be much more difficult to locate on 9X, and wobbles will be magnified as well. Save the highest power setting for sighting in or sniping pennies. Close or moving targets will be extremely difficult to locate. You'll be better served by dialing it down to 3X. If the need arises, you can always crank it up.

Eye relief: This is the distance from your eye to the ocular lens at which a full image is obtained. It's the same spot where the exit pupil is at full diameter. Many scopes will have eye relief running between 3-4 inches. You wouldn't think an inch of variance could make much difference, but it can – especially if your scope is mounted to the outer limits. A position change or thick winter clothing can introduce problems. I mount scopes to see a full image at maximum magnification, while wearing the appropriate clothing. Eye relief will probably decrease as magnification increases. You may also see a change when shooting prone. Suddenly, your eye may be too close. Adequate eye relief is essential when shooting high-powered rifles, which produce substantial recoil. You don't want that ocular lens housing to ram your eye. Personal style plays a large part in the equation. I shoot fairly head-up, and shop for generous eye relief models running 4 inches or more. I wouldn't want a tall shooter to fire one of my harder-kicking centerfires, since an injury could result.

Here's one way to instantly adjust eye-relief without affecting zero: an adjustable stock.
This one is part of S&W's 15-22 MOE model.

Clearance is less of an issue with low-recoil rimfires, but they can cause other problems. The small receivers are often fairly short, which can sometimes pose difficulties during scope mounting. The spacing of the lens bells and turrets isn't always compatible with ring positions. Optimum eye relief, which is a personalized adjustment, may then be difficult to acquire. Very short scopes with tighter eye relief specs are the ones that may cause you grief. If in doubt, you may be ahead of the game by spending a few extra dollars at a full-line gun shop for your scope and its installation. They'll probably bore-sight it, too. It won't be an exact zero, but will put you on paper for final sighting in.

Focus: Most scopes have a threaded ocular housing to accommodate different shooters. By turning the rear lens, optimal focus can be achieved. Lately, fast-focus models have become popular. A quick twist of a separate outer ring produces gross movements, which can be referenced off simple "+ or –" setttings. The more traditional designs employ fine threads for movement of the whole rear assembly. I like them because a locking ring can be cinched up to maintain my setting. Younger shooters might have trouble seeing my crosshairs. Shared users would probably want a fast-focus design, which should be checked for divergent shot groups.

Focus is achieved by aiming at the sky (or a blank wall), while adjusting the scope until the reticle is sharp. PA models should be set to infinity and focused on their highest setting. However, I've sometimes re-focused a non-PA centerfire model for close-range use by first aiming at a target. It helped at short airgun distances of 10-20 yards, but was a hindrance at normal ranges.

When backing the scope's ocular bell out, be careful not to go too far. It will probably have a stop, but I'd rather be safe than sorry. You won't want to break its seal or introduce recoil hazards.

Adjustable everything: Variable power, target turrets, and parallax. It's great for sniping tiny targets, but probably more than we need in the bush.

A closer look at target turrets with their protective caps removed. The numbered graduations indicate MOA. The finer tick-marks are ¼ MOA.

Turrets and MOA: You'll see the "minute-of-angle" term often. It's really just an angular measurement representing 1/60th of a degree. Since each circle has 360 degrees, there are 21,600 minutes of angle within it (360 x 60). We'll need to know this information because many scopes and dot sights are graduated accordingly. As often as not, their elevation and windage turrets are marked in MOA increments (while others may use inches).

Fortunately, we can keep things fairly simple. As it turns out, 1 MOA equals roughly 1 inch at 100 yards (1.047 to be exact). If your turrets are graduated in ¼ MOA increments, 4 clicks should equate to a reticle adjustment of 1-inch at 100 yards.

The ¼ MOA scale is fairly common, but some low-magnification sights use ½ MOA settings. Conversely, high-magnification target or varmint scopes often employ fine 1/8 MOA adjustments. As long as you can reference everything from 100 yards, it's easy to extrapolate other ranges. One MOA equals two inches at 200 yards and ½-inch at 50 yards. If you're fortunate enough to own a "MOA" rifle, it will be accurate enough to place its shots within these measurements.

Some people brag that their rifle will shoot one MOA at 100 yards. Well, it may also do that at 200 or even 400 yards. In that case, groups should run around 2 and 4 inches (although reality may dictate variances).

Some reticles are also MOA-calibrated. Dot sights often use this term to describe the subtension (coverage) of the aiming point. A 4-MOA dot will subtend roughly 4 inches at 100 yards.

Reticles: The old, original set of thin, bisecting crosshairs has been supplanted by a duplex-type reticle. The centermost sections remain thin, but each outer portion is thicker. The result is a more visible reticle that works better in reduced light. Other designs are becoming more common, and some use circles or diamonds. Illuminated reticles are offered by many scope manufacturers, and many use a larger 30mm scope tube to accommodate the circuitry. Intensity can be controlled by an extra rheostat knob, which introduces more complexity as well as the need for batteries.

The latest rage involves holdover aiming reticles and trajectory compensating turrets. Plenty of variations exist, which we'll explore momentarily. Trajectory compensating turrets use a calibrated elevation turret with scaled graduations that correspond to a bullet's path.

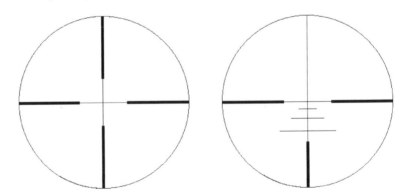

Two reticle examples: The duplex (L), and a generic rendition of a ballistic-aiming system. Hopefully, its fine horizontal lines will correspond with useful yardage increments.

I'd be leery of lower-priced scopes with a turret feature. The internals may be plastic and subject to early wear.

On the other hand, scopes with holdover reticles are relatively simple, and are my personal preference. Usually, they are designed to work on the highest magnification, with specific bullet weights and velocities. Most have crosshairs with Mil-dots, descending horizontal yardage lines, or circles as part of the reticle. The shooter aligns the appropriate aiming point with the target, thus compensating for the bullet's trajectory. Centerfire versions may have aiming points graduated in 100-yard increments, good for shots of 500 yards or more. Rimfire versions may have shorter increments useable to 150 or 200 yards (quite a stretch for a .22 LR).

A Mil-dot is used to compute range against target size for lead and holdover. You'll see this system more often on large centerfire tactical scopes. Holdover lines or circles are more common on rimfire models, and will theoretically coincide with specific loads. Don't be surprised if the aiming points don't exactly match claimed yardages. The way to know is to shoot groups at measured distances. If they don't match up, you can still use them. Just figure out the actual ranges where your bullets and aiming points coincide, or note the claimed distance discrepancies. Have some fun shooting at extended ranges from a good rest or bipod, and affix this data to your rifle with a label. You'll need to shoot with the scope set to its maximum magnification, or errors will occur.

Actually, you can sometimes use less magnification to offset discrepancies. I drop down two powers on a short-barreled .223 varmint rig, which loses some velocity. The ballistic reticle is indexed for faster bullets, but lines up out to 500 yards by using this trick.

Lacking any reference lines, it's still possible to wing it with a duplex reticle. This design has thin inner crosshairs with thicker outer sections. The uppermost part of the thick bottom post will coincide with your bullet's strike at *some* distance. Once you figure out the actual yardage, you can use it as a makeshift long-range aiming point.

Parallax adjustment? You don't absolutely need it. Again, you can shop for a non-adjustable rimfire calibrated scope. It will probably be a smaller package, and one easier to use. In fact, you can get by with a centerfire scope if it is properly mounted. Your eye should comfortably center on the ocular (or rear) lens to capture a full field of view. In other words, you shouldn't need to hunt for the full image. With centered viewing, parallax errors will be mostly eliminated, especially at lower magnifications. So again, mounting plays a pivotal role, as do stock design and consistent position.

Rimfire rifles chambered for .22 WMR or .17 HMR will work well with centerfire scopes. Buy one factory-set for 100 yards. Sure, you *can* choose a PA model, but it's not absolutely necessary. A non-PA 3-9 should work just fine.

Everybody seems to think a variable scope like a 3-9 needs to be cranked all the way up and left at 9X. For most uses it doesn't! My big game scopes are carried on 3X, and any .22 LR versions spend much time on 5X.

DOT SIGHTS

Most are electronic, containing an illuminated diode that is housed within a tube. The shooter sees a red or green dot, which is superimposed on the target from an internal prism. Some designs also display circles, crosshairs, or even selectable options. A rheostat may permit the user to regulate the dot's intensity for varying light conditions. A few units like Trijicon's Reflex Sight don't use electricity at all. Instead, either ambient light or a radioactive Tritium lamp are used to illuminate an internal fiber-optic element.

A 5-shot group fired with the author's old Remington M-510 bolt-action at 50 yards. The scope is a very basic Bushnell fixed 4X .22 model. It's simple and it works with good ammo, in this case .22 LR Federal Gold Medal Target.

Design: Confusion seems to exist between dot sights and lasers. Each is a totally different design, the laser projecting an external and concentrated beam of red or green light. A dot sight's aiming point is strictly internal and visible only within the sight body. Some designs incorporate both features, the laser being externally added to the dot sight tube. A good example is Redfield's latest "CounterStrike", which mounts to Picatinny rails.

With dot sights, typically no magnification is involved, field of view is huge, and eye relief is a non-issue. In other words, they're fast to get on target. The dot's size is typically expressed in minutes-of-angle. A 6.5 MOA dot will cover roughly 6 ½ inches at 100 yards. At 300 yards, it will cover nearly 20 inches. This size is good for close-quarter shooting, but small targets will be hard to hit because they can disappear behind the dot. I don't like them for all-around use, but for close and fast shooting, they're just the ticket. A 2 MOA dot is my personal preference, providing a nice balance of speed and precision. However, it's not the right choice for tiny targets or those at long range. For those, you'll

The full gamut of dot sights, price-wise. The Aimpoint (top) costs more than $400.The little Burris Fast-Fire sells for roughly half of that and the others are proportionally less.

need a scope. An adjustable parallax feature isn't offered or needed. You can buy auxiliary magnifying units that mount behind them. They're fairly expensive and increase overall size to that of a scope.

Options: The quality centerfire dot sights are also expensive, costing as much as a decent scope. We used an inventory of Trijicon Reflex sights for many years with good results. We have since switched to a greater number of Aimpoint "Patrol" electronic sights, which are working well on our AR-15 carbines. Battery life is phenomenal, but either type costs $400 or more.

On a .22, which doesn't generate much recoil and may be subject to casual use, one can spend less. Dot intensity is usually adjustable, and many types provide red or green color choices. Since these units run on batteries, you'll want a few spares. My S&W AR-22 has a small storage compartment built into its grip and it serves this purpose well. I paid only $65 for the Walther dot sight, and it seems perfect on this rifle. For fast work on falling plates, it's hard to beat this compact package. If my life depended on it, though, I'd spend more!

S&W 15-22 with an inexpensive Walther dot-sight. It's still working after several years.

Very small, tubeless sights are becoming more popular. They resemble miniature pre-flat-screen TV sets, and are extremely compact. Most, but not all, require dismounting during battery changes. Afterwards, you'll need a new zero. I have three generations of Burris Fast-Fire sights, and the latest FF-III solves this problem. The battery compartment has been relocated topside, permitting easy changes. Still, at over $200, it may not appeal to everyone. I drafted my first-generation unit for use on a .22 target pistol. One problem with the miniature designs is accumulation of water during wet conditions. The "screen" won't accept typical lens caps used for tube sights, and not every make is waterproof. Still, I like them because of their small size.

Dot sight mounting: Dot sights are great for plinking. They also keep overall rifle weight down. Electronics can fail, and the lower-priced models will more than likely quit at some point. That said, I have a 20-year-old Tasco Pro Point that is still going strong on a Ruger 10/22. It has a 30mm tube and is mounted in Warne QD rings, which actually do repeat zero. Switching between the dot sight and a scope only takes a few seconds. The scope has a ballistic reticle, and is also mounted in Warne QD rings. Both sets detach by turning levers, and are designed to mount on common Weaver-type bases.

Two different sighting systems for one rifle, thanks to Warne 1" and 30mm QD rings. Surprisingly, they maintain zero very well..

One thing to keep in mind is that many of the miniature sights have Weaver/Picatinny-type bases. By using a single dovetail adapter, you should be able to mount one to a grooved receiver. Check out the B-Square (or similar Hawke) adapters meant for grooved receivers. They slip over the dovetail cuts and, after tightening with two side-mounted cap screws, provide a Weaver surface. They're slick little units that won't mar the rifle.

Batteries: Since most of these sights depend on batteries, it's worth having a few spares on hand. They'll all die at some point, and one common cause is

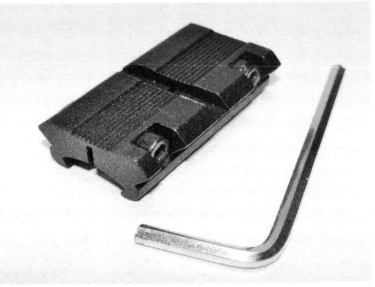

B-Square's adapter converts a grooved receiver to a Weaver-type base. The smallest dot-sights will only require one.

operator error. Although their lowest settings are useful in dim light, a faint dot is easy to miss after sunup. I've put more than one away when it was still turned on.

OPTICAL SIGHT CARE

Remember that sealed interior? The scope's integrity must be preserved, so don't try taking one apart! This could happen inadvertently if excessive adjustments were applied. The windage and elevation turrets should have adjustment stops. Don't force them as they approach their limits, or you'll break the scope. If you run out of adjustment, something is probably wrong with your mounting setup. Improper cleaning can scratch a lens or wear off its coating. Resist the urge to use a glove or shirt to wipe off condensation. A light fogging from your breath, followed by a clean soft patch is safer. Eyeglass cleaning systems are better and Leupold sells a "Lens Pen". A good set of scope covers is worth having in the long run.

Good insurance: a set of protective lens caps.

Dot sight batteries can cause problems related to handling and our natural oils in fingerprints. We're careful to avoid touching their surfaces during installation. They also need periodic inspection to detect any leakage. Again, you'll want spare batteries. Even with limited use, it's only a matter of time until a sight is inadvertently left on.

Chapter 7

CHOOSING YOUR SIGHTING SYSTEM

W e'll need some means to aim our rifle. The chosen system will depend upon our intended use. For those whose primary interest lies in eliminating rats from a barn, a basic .22 rimfire with factory-issued open sights will do. Casual plinkers often employ the same system, limiting their targets to cans at relatively close range. Open sights are fast and lots of fun on dancing targets. A receiver (or peep) sight provides more precision, and is a fairly affordable improvement. Shooters intent on wringing out maximum accuracy will be shopping for a scope.

IRON SIGHTS

Those shooters opting to stay with open sights should check out the types sold by Williams. Matching front and rear sights are offered for the more popular rifles like Ruger's 10/22. Fiber-optic versions are especially popular, and Williams offers "Fire Sights'" with high-visibility elements installed. Marbles and Lyman also sell iron sights.

Depending on your ability, gunsmith installation may be safest. In other cases, installation may as simple as loosening a screw. One improvement I make is the installation of a green fiber-optic front sight. A common open sight mounting method is a 3/8" dovetail cross slot, machined into the barrel by the factory. Sometimes, both the front and rear sights are mounted this way. Exchanging a sight

requires drifting out the old one, normally, from left to right (as viewed while aiming). A factory sight can be tough to remove, so caution will be necessary to prevent a dinged barrel. A small brass hammer helps, but a sight pusher tool is better. That's why a trip to a good gunsmith is advised.

RECEIVER SIGHTS

Williams sells a line of receiver sights to fit many models. Their M-52 GRS will slip over the grooves of most .22 rifles. Lyman, XS Outdoors, and Skinner also sell some interesting peep sights. I've used them all with positive results. You'll often need a taller front sight, due to the higher design of the rear. Some rifles, like the pricier Marlins, have factory-installed

Williams rear sight with fiber-optic elements..

Choosing Your Sighting System | 97

folding open rear sights. The blade can just be pivoted down for receiver or scope sighting options. Another solution is to drift out the rear sight and install a filler blank in its slot. I have several rifles equipped with receiver sights and fiber-optic front beads. They're simple and weatherproof. Most of the apertures present a "ghost-ring" sight picture. I normally ditch the supplied removable disk that has a small aiming hole, in favor of the sight's threaded housing. The large hole may not seem very precise, but the results on a target can be surprising. I've shot a number of sub-two-inch 100-yard groups from a Marlin .45/70 and Remington .308, equipped with this arrangement. When heavy, wet snow is clinging to spruce boughs, they make a great choice. A companion rimfire is lots of fun, and provides economical off-hand practice.

XS Sights small and rugged peep sight, mounted on a Marlin.

The addition of a peep-sight may require a taller front sight
like the one on the bottom Marlin barrel.

SCOPES

For maximum aiming precision, a scope will be necessary. For consistent results, it will need to be a decent one. Please don't cheap out, and be sure to buy a scope with a one-inch tube. The little 7/8" blister pack models are nothing special, and will probably have plastic lenses. Going to the other extreme, large scopes with big 50 mm objective lenses can be problematic. They add unnecessary weight, and also require higher rings. Close-range hits become more difficult, as does a proper check weld. Maybe I'm overly fussy, but a too-high scope really drives me nuts. Solid head contact with a stock is something I need for effective shooting. That rules out see-through scope rings geared towards fast iron sight use. Again, an eye centered behind the scope helps eliminate parallax problems. If funds are tight, try to find a .22 LR model that is parallax corrected for shorter ranges. A fixed 4X is a simple design that can be sold for less money. High rollers might buy a variable-power PA model.

The top pick: Leupold's Rimfire Series: In this case, we're talking about three different scopes. Two, a straight 4x and 2x7, are factory adjusted for rimfire parallax. Both are compact units that look sharp on twenty-two rifles. The third is a 3x9 Parallax Adjustable Compact, which is somewhat larger but not excessively top-heavy. You'll pay more for these, but you won't be disappointed. On a smaller sporting rifle, I'd go with the 4X or 2-7X models. They are properly proportioned and will save a bit of weight. A larger, more precise rifle like a heavy-barreled bolt-action or custom Ruger 10/22 deserves the 3x9 AO.

The hotter .17 HMR or .22 WMR rifles are useful at longer ranges, so a conventional scope will work just fine. Leupold's "Rifleman" series is the starting point for these. The grades advance to VX-I, VX-II, VX-III, and beyond. Those with ballistic aiming reticles can be employed to extend useful range. Recently, Leupold resurrected the old Redfield line. These scopes are built to compete with cheaper brands, but quality production is still assured. Although prices are less, the Redfield scopes represent great value.

Burris Timberline: At one point, Burris had a line of dedicated rimfire/airgun scopes. I still have several adjustable-objective models in 6, 3x9 and 4x12. They're well-proportioned, with plenty of eye relief. The 4x12 seems touchy at full power, but works well at 10X or below. That's plenty of magnification for most rimfire shooting. The 6X Compact is actually enough glass for paintballs out to 50 yards. If you stumble on to any of these scopes, Burris will still service them. Meanwhile, they now list a 4.5x14 Timberline, which has an AO and Ballistic-Plex reticle.

The Burris 4.5-14 x 32mm is relatively compact, but has several useful features such as an adjustable objective lens and trajectory-compensating reticle.

The size is not too large, and the internal holdover lines are useful at further ranges. The Magnum shooters could choose a 3x9 Timberline, or Full-Field II.

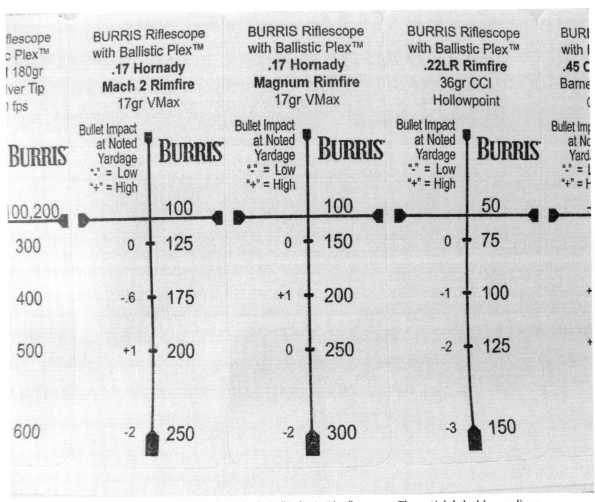

Burris includes adhesive labels with their "Balistic Plex" scopes. The reticle's hold-over lines coincide with different yardages, dictated by caliber-specific trajectories.

Nikon: Several rimfire specific models are listed, which cover most bases. Prices are reasonable and features are good. Their 3x9 Pro-Staff Target EFR has an adjustable objective. A smaller, straight 4X is parallax corrected for 50 yards. In between are some 2X7s. They're a solid value. My son has used a 3x9 on his .17 HMR to raise havoc on our local crow population.

Cabela's: I recently bought a 3-9x40mm "Caliber Specific Scope". I chose their .22 LR model, but .22 WMR and .17 HMR versions are also sold. Two variants are offered and one uses calibrated turrets for range-compensating adjustments. The model I bought uses an "EXT Bullet Drop Reticle" with graduated holdover lines instead. No external parallax adjustment feature is offered with this scope and the built-in setting isn't listed. The unit is fairly large and looks a lot like a Bushnell Banner. One thing it has in common is a surprisingly bright and clear image, especially considering its $100 price. I mounted mine on an accurate, custom Ruger 10/22 for evaluation. A series of 50-yard groups were then fired at 3, 6, and 9 power settings. Only a very small shift was noted on the lowest setting, constituting less than 0.3" at 50 yards. After zeroing on 9X at 50 yards, more 75 and 100-yard groups were fired with Winchester 37 grain Super-X HPs. The bullets struck a bit high. Re-zeroing with slower 40 grain Federal Gold Medal Target rounds, the system worked perfectly. For the money, it seems like a good buy. In order to use the holdover reticle, the scope must be set on its maximum magnification. As long as you remember that, the system is pretty intuitive. Others may prefer the calibrated elevation turret version, applying clicks for dead-center aiming. One concern I have with any lower-cost scope is its long-term consistency when moving parts are involved.

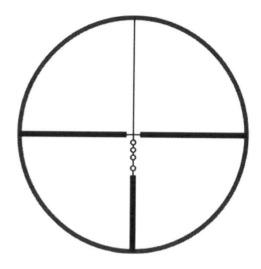

Nikon's BDC Reticle comes in different versions calibrated to specific calibers including rimfires. Determine the range and hold accordingly, using the calibrated circle.

Cabelas 3x9 Caliber-specific Scope" has an "EXT Bullet Drop Reticle" calibrated for .22 LR trajectories. Nevertheless, shoot it at various distances to verify the results.

DOT SIGHTS

Choices abound, but many have Weaver/Picatinny-type bases. Again, a B-Square or Hawke adapter will slip over the dovetail cuts and provide a Weaver base conversion.

High-end miniaturized dots are sold by Trijicon, Leupold, and others. You'll pay more for the sights than you will for many rimfire rifles. Since battlefield conditions won't be a concern, we can do a bit better price-wise. Here are just a few:

Burris Fast-Fire: This small sight has gone through three evolutions, and I have them all. The FF-III is the most user-friendly, but it's also the most expensive at around $250. Like the somewhat simpler and less expensive FF-II, its main attribute is very compact size. Unlike the FF-III, it'll need to be dismounted for battery changes. The FF-II has a 4 MOA red dot and friction adjustments. The FF-III has a slightly finer 3 MOA dot with click-stops and an intensity adjustment. They all run on a CR-2032 coin-type battery. The original FF-I isn't waterproof, but the others are.

The compact Burris Fast-Fire III. Like many such sights it's designed for a Picatinny-type base. It'll go on a B-Square adapter with some minor tinkering.

Redfield Accelerator: Here's another small sight, similar to the Burris. It has a larger 6 MOA dot with L, M, H, and Auto intensity settings. It also runs off a CR-2032 battery that can be replaced without dismounting the unit. An adapter is available that permits mounting of the Redfield to the bases of some other manufacturers' units. Grooved or 11mm dovetails may still be problematic, but a conversion base can solve this problem. Cost is $200, with a "no excuses" warranty.

Bushnell First Strike: This sight presents a viable alternative for a few small sacrifices in features. The 5 MOA dot runs on an auto-adjust sensor. Unlike the Burris and Redfield units, it has no on/off switch. Instead, replacement of its plastic cover shuts the Bushnell off. Replacement of the CR-2032 battery requires disassembly and re-zero, but like the others, this sight is waterproof. It also comes with an AR-15 riser block. The warranty is one year, but the price is only $110.

Konus Atomic: Unlike the miniature TV-types, this one has a tubular body. However, it's not a whole lot bigger. I have one mounted to a combination gun, and the Atomic has so far withstood its not-quite-nuclear 12-gauge recoil. A side-mounted dial permits five different intensity settings, in choices of red or green dot colors. An "off" setting powers down the 4 MOA dot. The unit is only around 2 ½ inches long, and weighs less than 4 ounces. It runs off a CR-2032 battery. One neat item included with the Atomic is a B-Square adapter. My Finnish combo gun has an 11mm rail. The adapter slips right on and provides a Weaver-type mounting conversion that matches this sight. The Atomic should also fit behind its magazine, at the rear of the receiver. I bought mine from Midway USA several years ago, and it's still listed for around $100 with a limited lifetime warranty.

The Konus Atomic, which comes with a B-Square rimfire adapter. Look closely and you'll see a second, which was added as a spacer.

Bushnell: The TRS-25 looks very similar to the Atomic, but has a 3 MOA red dot. It also shares the same dimensions (and battery), so it's very compact. Cost is around $100 and it comes with a 2-year warranty.

Bushnell, among others, also sells a line of larger tube-type dot sights that mount in standard scope rings. By selecting the right set, you could mount one directly to a grooved receiver.

PACKAGE GUNS

You can buy "package guns", which come with a scope and mounts. They are available in centerfire, rimfire, and airgun versions. The firearm packages typically come pre-assembled, but some airgun versions just contain separately boxed components that require user assembly. Regardless, such combinations are often marketed towards lower price points. An economy .22 rifle package may provide utility, but it won't necessarily be ready to use right out of the box. The eye relief may be wrong simply because it has been generically set at the factory. It will only be bore-sighted at best, and a few we tried were way off the mark. We've also seen some come through with canted cross-hairs. In other words, there is a good chance that the shooter will still need to perform some of the steps explained below.

SYSTEM SETUP

Most of the following process applies to scopes. Most dot sights, particularly those marketed for rimfires, lack sophisticated mounting systems. Assuming they can be adapted to a rimfire, you just slap them on and hope for the best. Many will sight in, due to large tubes with wide ranges of reticle adjustments. Often, a scope can be mounted without difficulties as well. However, I've run into problems more than once. It's worth understanding the ins and outs, particularly if a centerfire rifle is in your future. For those less adventuresome, a trip to a full-service gun shop should result in a useful setup that will get you on paper. It won't be final-zeroed though, just bore-sighted. You'll still need to make some final live-fire adjustments.

Mounts: Even the better sets won't break the bank. Many centerfire systems employ two major components consisting of mounting bases and scope rings. The bases are screwed to a drilled and tapped receiver, and separate rings hold the scope. However, those rimfire shooters with grooved receivers can use a set of "tip-off" rings that serve both purposes. Some rimfire receivers even include both options.

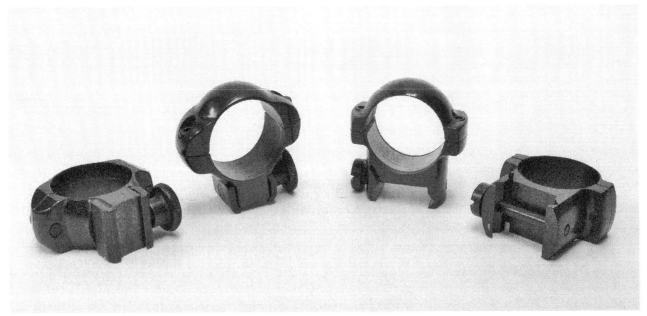

Redfield's 1" tip-off rings (L) will clamp directly to most rimfire grooved receivers. The Burris Zee-Rings (R) are meant for a Weaver or Picatinny-type base.

Regardless of your system, shop for heights permitting proper head-to-stock placement. Many of the cheapest rings are made from pot metal, with metric cap screws. For a few more dollars, I've had good luck with steel Leupold, Redfield, or Burris one-inch tipoffs. The Millett windage-adjustable rings require some tinkering, but will clamp on American or European dovetails. I use two sets of Warne QD rings on a custom 10/22. They mount on a "Power" Picatinny-type base and repeat zero fairly well, permitting use of either a scope or dot sight. These rings all look sharp, and will really dress up your rifle.

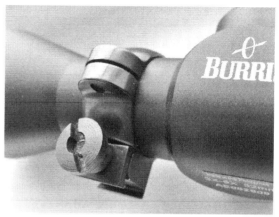

The Burris tip-off rings are another nicely made, all-steel alternative.

A "Power" Picatinny base mounted on a Ruger 10/22, with Warne "Maxima" QD rings.

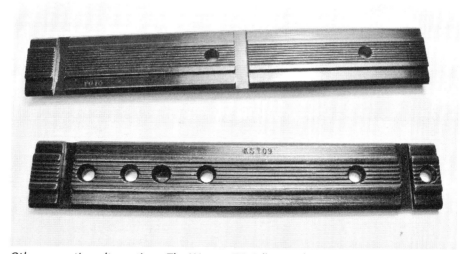

Other mounting alternatives: The Weaver TO-9 (bottom) mounts on a standard Ruger 10/22 receiver. It will then accept either Weaver-type rings or tip-offs. The Weaver T-10 slips on to grooved receivers and converts them to a Weaver base pattern.

Bolt-action rifles will need enough height to provide bolt handle clearance during opening. Regardless of the action, a scope's forward bell shouldn't contact the barrel. Big target turrets look cool, but can interfere with ejection, causing semi-auto stoppages.

Millett's "Angle-Lock" tip-off rings permit windage adjustments by the use of opposing claws.
This medium-height set provides adequate bolt clearance.

Bottom line: not every mount and scope will work with every rifle. In the end, it will probably be a whole lot less aggravating to buy from that full-line shop. You might pay a bit more initially, but then again, you won't have to deal with questionable opened mail order exchanges. If you're not in a rush, they may even do the setup.

Safety first! Before any hands-on work begins, we need a safe area for muzzle management. Remember, treat all guns as if they're loaded! Check and then double-check for the presence of any live ammunition and make it go away. The upcoming safety Chapter provides more information, and should be referenced before going any further.

Scope mounting: Position the rings to provide adequate eye relief, with wide tube spacing for better support. It's best to maintain a tiny gap between the rings, scope turret, and bell. A power selector ring also needs a bit of clearance. Things work best if the rings are first loosely assembled for fine tuning. The better sets are often machined from one piece, so their tops should remain indexed. You can indicate each with penciled reference lines, prior to disassembly.

Once everything is roughly lined up, snug the screws enough to maintain slight scope movement. That way, you'll have latitude for final eye relief and reticle leveling. To acquire the former, assume a natural shooting position. A variable scope should be on maximum power. Slide it until a full image is barely obtained. It's worth setting that distance with clothing appropriate for anticipated weather conditions.

Leveling can be maddening at times. I perform this chore on low power when finalizing variable scopes. The larger field of view helps, especially if the image is far from my eye. I'll sometimes place the muzzle on a soft floor and reference the crosshairs off action surfaces. Aligning them with horizontal or vertical edges also helps. Roofs and wall corners work when aiming. The best bet is to use levels. You can buy special sets or use a small bubble-level, referencing off the elevation cap and part of the rifle. That's sometimes easier said than done. I'm okay with getting a second or third opinion. You'll need level crosshairs, especially with ballistic aiming reticles,. Otherwise, windage errors will develop when the lower holdover lines are used.

Screws should be firmly tightened using a correct parallel-ground bit. Allen or Torx-type heads are becoming popular. These systems work fine, as long as the correct bits are selected. A rimfire won't generate too much recoil, but mounts can creep over time. Loss of zero is a possible clue. Overtightening can damage a scope tube or strip the screw holes. As always, there is a happy balance. I use a tiny dab of blue threadlocker on bases, but never on rings. Each ring screw is alternately tightened in a sequence, to maintain uniform gaps between the bottom and top ring halves.

Even an experienced shooter can goof up the actual mounting job. We've seen scopes mounted backwards, and others rotated 90 degrees out. The elevation turret should be on top! The windage turret will then protrude off the right side of the action. Recheck everything before burning some powder. Once in a while, a scope can rotate a bit during final tightening. The whole process can be trial and error, so earmark adequate time.

Mechanical zero: Ideally, the scope should zero somewhere near the center of its adjustment range and any gross corrections should be made with the mounts. A number of centerfire systems employ windage-adjustable bases, but rimfire mounts designed for grooved receivers generally lack this feature. Millett "Angle-Loc" rings are an exception, and can be centered via opposing clamps. Other manufacturers like Leupold and Burris sell well-built centerfire-type systems for some rimfire rifles with drilled and tapped receivers. If you use them, it's worth centering the scope's adjustments first. To determine the centers of each turret's range, carefully dial each in one direction until it stops. Then move it in the opposite direction through its entire range, counting revolutions and clicks. At that point, come back halfway and you should be centered. If you use an adjustable mounting system, you can then get your gross windage fairly close. A brand new scope should come out of its packaging already centered. Anything goes with a used scope and sometimes, as we gain experience, we decide to switch one out. Once the adjustments are centered, look for a rotating reference scale encircling the knob. You may see numbers, including a "0". If possible, carefully align that with a small witness mark. It'll help later on…

A Picatinny base (top) with generic Weaver-type rings. The Redfield set (bottom) is most often seen on centerfire sporting rifles. Note the turn-in dovetailed front and windage-adjustable rear rings.

Bore sighting: How will you know when your scope is "close"? Well, a rifle with a removable bolt can permit a visual means for rough alignment. The process is called "bore sighting". Using a bolt-action as an example, you can secure the rifle in a couple of U-shaped recesses, cut into the opposing sides of a cardboard box. If the bolt is removed, you can sight through the breech end of the barrel and align it with a distant object. In a pinch, I've used a neighbor's chimney cap or a fence post top, although a round object is better. The exact distance isn't critical, but something 50-100

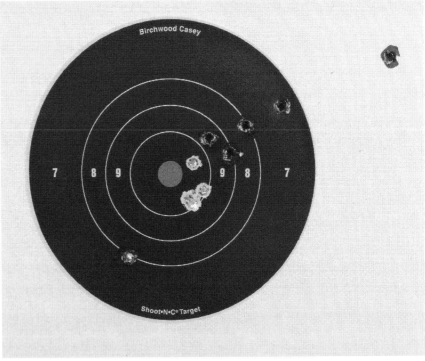

The high right outside shot was the first bore-sighted hit, fired at 100 yards. Adjustments were then made using scope turrets. The final group isn't blackened.

yards away is helpful. After the object appears centered in the barrel, you can carefully note the location of your reticle. Hopefully, it won't diverge too badly. With an adjustable-type mount, you should be able to come left or right as needed. Once close, you can then dial the scope turrets to get centered on the target. Most rimfire systems don't have this feature, meaning all adjustments will need to occur through the scope turrets alone. With care, you can often place the first shot within 3-5" of a 100-yard bullseye (better to start at 25 yards though).

If things don't line up, you can sometimes switch the locations of your front and rear rings. More than likely, though, you'll need a different set. Most systems lack an elevation feature, meaning shims are in order. At that point, for many people, a trip to a gunsmith will be forthcoming. It's worth having a closely centered reticle when possible. Those shooters near the extreme limits may not be able to sight in with different loads, or at greater ranges. The actual image can appear off-center as well.

One thing to keep in mind is that your adjustment scales will work backwards when maintaining bore and target alignment. The easy fix is a switch to centered crosshairs on the target. The bore will then be off-target, just as it would during live-fire. The only problem is that the target may be hard to locate though a small caliber barrel during major adjustments. That's why I first align the bore with the target. If the scope is really out of whack, it's just easier to tell.

With closed actions like a Ruger 10/22, this trick won't work. In that case, you'll need a special bore-sighting instrument, which most gun shops keep on hand. Or, just shoot it at 25 yards! In fact, that's probably what most folks will do. Most rimfire ammo is less expensive than centerfire rounds, which can easily cost a dollar per shot. Burning though a half box of .22 LR is less disturbing. Still, it can be aggravating to discover your system won't line up when you're far from a set of tools.

SUMMARY

Here's the big thing to remember: Bore-sighting is NOT your last step. People often buy package guns, or pay a gunsmith to install and bore-sight a firearm, and then head into the woods. This is a huge mistake, likely to result in wounded game! The ONLY way we'll know for certain if our bullets will strike their intended spot is to do some serious shooting. We'll do some in a moment after reviewing safe gun handling.

Sources: More often than not, I find myself checking websites for specifications and costs. The actual manufacturers are your best bet for critical dimensions related to scopes and mounting systems. Since most optics companies don't sell direct to consumers, I often check Cabela's, Midway USA, Brownell's, Graf & Sons, Natchez, SWFA, and Optics Planet. And, again, your local gun shop is a good bet. You might pay a bit more up front, but you'll be assured of a functional scope and mounting system. Remember, not all combinations will work. Mail-ordered returns are a hassle, and can quickly undermine any hoped for savings.

CHAPTER 8

PRE-FIRE SAFETY REVIEW

This topic is covered more thoroughly in *"Survival Guns: A Beginner's Guide"*. In essence, by following a few basic rules at all times, we should be able to safely handle and fire any type of gun without endangering ourselves or others. Particularly in the case of a .22 rimfire, third parties are a concern. Sure, it's "only a twenty-two", but cemeteries are full of hapless victims who succumbed to a small 40 grain bullet. Not only will one carry a mile or more at maximum elevation, but it will return to earth with lethal force. Just stapling a target to a cardboard box without a proper back-stop is completely reckless. Even a .22 CB Cap has enough power to penetrate a human skull or chest cavity. The same is true for airgun projectiles, which claim lives every year. Handling any type of firearm or airgun warrants the upmost attention to a cardinal set of rules!

What goes up will come down. A safe backstop is essential!

THE UNIVERSAL SAFETY RULES

Don't attempt to fire a shot until these five "Universal Firearms Safety Rules" can be recited by heart.

#1: Treat all firearms as if loaded! We don't care if the safety is on or not, or whether the gun is unloaded. It doesn't matter if the action is open or closed. It's *ALWAYS* loaded, and should never sweep any part of you, or anyone else!

#2: Don't allow the muzzle to sweep something you're unwilling to destroy! This rule *always* applies, whether during handling or in storage. While participating in organized civilian programs, we teach our shooters to utilize "safe range carry". The gun is unloaded and on "safe", with the action open. It is carried vertically, with its muzzle higher than any shooter's head. This is not a tactical carry, but provides a safe start for new shooters. On a range, vertical racks are useful. Stow your gun with its action open, and watch your head when you retrieve it. Further caution will be necessary when using a sling. If carried muzzle-up, it's easy to sweep others while bending forward, and a careless rearward dismount can produce the same effect. Be aware of your muzzle at all times!

#3: Keep your finger off the trigger until ready to fire! Find an index point on the gun. Typically, the trigger finger will be extended forward, parallel with the bottom of the receiver. You can disengage a safety while committing to fire, but the trigger is off limits until the gun is fully mounted. You can also bet that most "accidental" shootings are the result of a failure to follow this rule, as well as the others. The safety is never a substitute for sloppy muzzle discipline. YOU are the safety!

#4: Be sure of your target, and what is beyond it! Again, even a standard .22 LR will travel a mile or more. If you shoot it, you own it! An adequate backstop is essential. A few pieces of lumber won't work. We need to exercise situational awareness at all times and manage our muzzles accordingly.

#5: Check any type of gun upon handling it. Many bolt or break-action guns are easy to inspect since their chambers are exposed when the action is opened. Auto-loaders, lever-actions, and pumps are often a different matter. The small enclosed breech end of tubular rimfire magazines can be especially hard to see, so check them and then do it again. Proper gun etiquette dictates that a firearm should be passed to someone else unloaded and on "safe", with its action open. The recipient should immediately check it as well. Bottom line: if you don't know how a gun works, leave it alone!

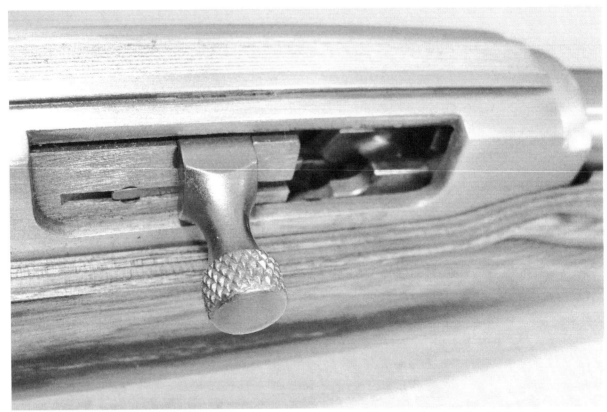

A tubular magazine action must be carefully scrutinized for safety's sake. Check it twice!

OTHER SAFETY CONCERNS

Especially with some tighter match-type chambers, an extractor can slip off the rim of a loaded cartridge, leaving it lodged in the barrel. The same situation can occur after inserting a .22 Long Rifle into a dirty chamber that has fired .22 Shorts. Besides the fact that you then have a loaded firearm in your hands, you'll need a way to safely clear it. Prying on the rim of any cartridge - particularly a rimfire type - is *not* recommended! The best bet is to point the gun in a safe direction and just shoot it. Worse case, you'd need a rod with an abundance of caution. I'd much prefer to fire it, at which point it'll probably eject. This is the safest fix for tightly-chambered aftermarket Ruger 10/22 barrels.

Squibs: If you detect a mild report, stop shooting, unload, leave the action open, and check for an obstruction. You might have just experienced an under-powered "squib-load". This can be a problem with low-velocity "Colibris", which can lodge a bullet in a rifle barrel due to friction. It's also not a bad idea to check a barrel if a gun has been in storage for a while.

Target hazards: Every year, careless people shoot themselves from ricocheting projectiles that bounce off tires, old TV screens, dense trees, or other makeshift targets. The lowest-velocity types, like CB Caps, are especially subject to this danger. Commercial steel reactive targets are safe with most .22 LR bullets if the manufacturer's cautions are followed. The hotter types, and Magnum loads, may dent them. At that point, such targets are unsafe with any projectile.

Common sense: It goes without saying that alcohol and drugs don't mix with firearms. Neither do unsupervised children or others who raise similar concerns. Unattended firearms are a huge problem, requiring responsible storage. Firearms safety and storage is covered in depth within the *Survival Guns* edition.

Lead: The discharge of conventional ammunition involves some exposure to lead. It's not only the primary material used for projectiles, but is also used in many priming mixtures.

Steel targets showing .22 LR hits. Wear safety glasses and maintain a safe distance of 25-yards or more. Check them for dents or dimples, too!

Many .22 loads use exposed lead bullets, as do airgun pellets. We all know that lead paint is a significant health hazard, something shooters should be mindful of as well. We can minimize concerns by shooting in well-ventilated areas and washing up afterwards. Perform any cleaning chores with similar precautions, away from your kitchen table!

Safety gear: Before firing a shot, track down a good set of shooting glasses and some hearing protection. Wear them any time firearms are discharged in your proximity, and make sure everyone else is properly equipped. Airgun projectiles can ricochet off things like trees, knock-down targets, or other types. Why risk losing an eye?

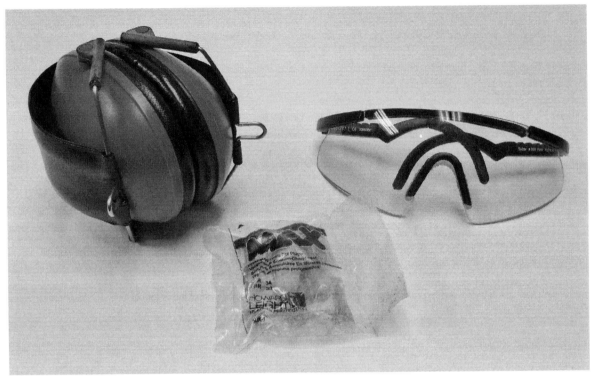

Essential safety gear. Safety glasses are a must and even a .22 will damage your hearing!

CHAPTER 9

ZERO and ACCURACY

At a recent tactical presentation, we were introduced to a new rifle which was pronounced "accurate". If ever there was an overused description, it had to be this one. I asked for specifics, but got vague replies. Since a sales pitch was in progress, I tried one more time. Would it shoot 1 MOA? As it turned out, the sales guy didn't really have a clue. He just parroted what he was told - it was "accurate".

Maybe I'm way too fussy about performance, but personally, I want to know what a rifle is capable of. And truthfully, with today's close-tolerance manufacturing, most shoot pretty well. Still, you'll never know for sure unless you take the time to find out. Now and then, you'll get a rude awakening. And even the most accurate rifle will be worthless if its barrel and aiming system don't coincide. So we face two chores: the first being to get on target, and the second being to find a usefully accurate load.

INITIAL ZERO

Before any serious accuracy testing commences, we'll need an approximate "zero". This term refers to aligning the sights with a target to ensure hits. The process is also known as "sighting in". Once completed, it should result in a system that places bullets where intended at a given distance. Minimizing human influences will be necessary to establish repeatable results, so a good stable rest is called for. Once a solid firing platform has been achieved, comparative loads can be properly evaluated. The winning combination can then be placed on target through adjustment of the sighting system.

Iron sight alignment using a "six o'clock hold", for precise aiming.

Iron sights: A good starting point is 25 yards. The target could be Birchwood Casey 4 ½" Shoot-N-C bullseye, which indicates each bullet hole by the appearance of a yellow border. Instead of aiming at its center, you may want to try a "six o'clock hold" on the bottom edge. It will provide a more precise aiming spot. You may opt for a smaller target, but it can actually get you in trouble. You'll need a clearly focused front sight to shoot irons accurately. A too-small bull can shift your focus to the target. The range and target size largely boil down to visual acuity.

Focus on your front sight and carefully squeeze the trigger from a good, solid rest. Fire at least 3 shots and then unload. Odds are good that some adjustments will be necessary. With iron sights, movements will be mostly trial and error. The rear sight will need to move in the same direction you want a bullet to go. Rear sights with stepped elevators are a bit less precise, but fairly convenient. Some others employ small screws. Windage (left and right) adjustments may require tapping of the rear sight in its barrel dovetail. A small pencil mark on each part can serve as a helpful reference. Don't use a steel hammer or you'll ding the barrel. A brass surface is better, with the gun firmly supported. Obviously, the right tools help. Those traveling long distances should make a little kit ahead of time.

Ideally, you'll eventually see a group form on top of your front sight, in the bottom of the bull. Once in a while, you may run into a system (like an AR-15) that requires movement of the front sight. In that case, your adjustments are backwards. The whole process is actually fairly simple if you think things through first. Just remember to properly clear the rifle before working on it!

Scopes and dot sights: If an optical sight is employed, two knobs will be used to adjust the crosshairs. They are located on a central turret housing, and each will be graduated to perform consistent movements in small increments. Many employ click-stops to regulate the process, each distinct click indicating a specific degree of movement. As mentioned previously, common value is "MOA", or minute of angle.

The fairly common ¼ MOA translates to roughly ¼" of adjustment at 100 yards. At 50 yards, this value would only be half of that, or 1/8", which can cause confusion to newer shooters. A set of directional arrows normally indicate the correct rotations, with "U" for up, or "R" for right. A rifle placing bullets below the target would need its elevation turret cranked up. A consistent series of shots is called a "group". If, say, a three-shot group was striking two inches low at 100 yards, a ¼ MOA elevation turret would need to come up 8 clicks. At 50 yards, 16 clicks would be needed.

An elevation turret showing click values and direction of movement. Dialing "up" 4 clicks should raise your point of impact approximately one inch at 100 yards.

During the initial range session, it's best to start closer. The odds are then better of capturing a bullet hole. If the first few rounds totally miss, then what? Randomly cranking the turrets is a recipe for frustration. There's nothing wrong with starting as close as 10 yards. I wouldn't back up any further than 25 yards for the first volley. Distance increments that permit easy adjustment calculations help. Using the same two-inch low example, you'd need to come up 32 clicks. If you have a rotating scale, you can align the "0" with the witness mark first, then carefully count each click.

A good, solid rest helps produce tight groups. There's nothing wrong with using a ruler to calculate the necessary clicks. Once you're on at 25 yards, you can back out to 50 yards. Your click values will then be 8 per inch, using this ¼ MOA example. Let's say you're now ¾" high and ½" right. You'll need to come down 6 clicks and left 4 clicks. Shoot at least 3 more shots to verify, then reset the scale to "0". Any further adjustments can thus be made without getting lost. Be sure to *carefully* reinstall the protective caps on the turrets. Most are fine-threaded, and they all need to go on straight.

Many turret knobs are cut to accept a dime, while others may have knurled edges. Not all have click-stops, relying on friction instead. Those that haven't been adjusted for a while can sometimes be stiff. You may even see one jump. This is more common with harder-kicking centerfire calibers, and can be maddening. Recoil suddenly jars the scope into its new adjustment setting, after the first or second shot. Not realizing this, you can go nuts adding extra clicks that must be subtracted later. One fix you can try is careful tapping of a turret, using a plastic screwdriver handle or scrap of wood. Don't beat it to death, just give it a couple light raps. I'd only do this if it seemed necessary.

The goal in the sighting-in stage is just to get a useful zero. From there, we can try a few different loads in the quest for optimum accuracy. An accurate rifle with decent optics, a solid rest, and proper technique are all required for best results. So is good ammunition!

RIMFIRE ACCURACY

For whatever reason, .22 rimfires seem to be downright finicky when it comes to ammunition preferences. We've seen weird things happen with both rifles and handguns.

Quirks: A friend had a Colt .22 revolver that should've been able to drive tacks. But at 50 feet, we were lucky to keep bullets on the paper. Many hit sideways, producing tell-tale keyholes. If you see those, *something* is seriously wrong. The whole gun seemed tight, so we were mystified. Things were looking grim until we threw in a cylinder full of Remington Thunderbolts, really just a plinking load. The ensuing group

A pretty 50-yard group fired from a Volquartsen .22 LR match-grade barrel. This custom Ruger 10/22 appears to like CCI Standard Velocity ammunition, but don't bet everything on only one group.

was the size of a quarter. The situation got even better from there. My buddy bought four bricks with the same lot number and his blood pressure returned to normal. Strange? You bet!

I've had good luck with Federal Gold Medal Target .22 Long Rifle in many handguns and rifles. But nothing is absolute, as witnessed by a custom Ruger 10/22 with a match grade Volquartsen barrel. Even lower-priced bulk-pack loads shot reasonably well, but I couldn't keep 10 Gold Medal shots on paper at 50 yards. I could actually see them wander off course through the scope. They looked like little missiles steered by drunken pilots. With open sights and the same rounds, thumbnail-sized groups were easy at 25 yards from my Marlin Model 60. A second VQ barrel was mounted to the same Ruger action, producing excellent accuracy with the same lot of ammunition. Go figure.

If you happened to blunder into a bad combination, you could drive yourself nuts while trying to sight in a rifle or when attempting to impress your buddies. You'd definitely wind up buying them lunch, which begs the question: what exactly does "accurate' mean? I will say that consistent 50-yard MOA (half-inch) .22 LR groups are pretty hard to come by. At least, they are in my experience.

Accuracy expectations: The best bet for achieving this standard is to go with a good bolt-action. A substantial progression of quality rifles has marched through my safe, including those built by Sako, Kimber, and Remington, just to name a few. After burning up several hundred dollars' worth of premium .22 ammo, I realized a true MOA .22 sporter was hard to come by. I could get close, but my hopes were always dashed by thorough testing. It was possible to average 5/8", but that last 1/8" was really elusive. My present Anschutz broke the barrier and is here to stay. In the end, it probably would've been cheaper to buy a $1500 Cooper and just be done with it (or living with that extra 1/8-inch, just shooting my old $90 Remington Model 510).

The accuracy ratings shown below are strictly my own, based on too many years spent chasing tiny groups.

Recommended sight-in distances and accuracy expectations with rimfire rifles				Average groups	
Cartridge	Zero & range	Rds per group	Groups per load	Good	Great
.22 LR Bulk	50 yards	5 rounds	5 each (25 rds)	1.00"	0.75"
.22 LR Target	50 yards	5 rounds	5 each (25 rds)	0.65"	0.50"
.22 Magnum	100 yards	5 rounds	5 each (25 rds)	1.25"	1.00"
.17 HMR	100 yards	5 rounds	5 each (25 rds)	1.00"	0.75"
Average of five, 5-shot groups from sandbag rests, fired carefully in calm conditions					

Those not seriously into shooting may wonder what difference a half-inch would matter. Well, it might not matter much at all, depending on the intended use of a rifle. If the primary objective involves dispatching garden-raiding critters at close range, who cares? On the other hand, if you value performance, you'll want to quantify the capabilities of what you own. As I mentioned previously, the great accuracy of the .17 HMR has permitted some really tricky shots. I'd otherwise never attempt them, but the bigger picture, at least for me, is the integration of precision rimfire shooting with centerfire rifle work.

Small reactive .22 targets can really improve your overall rifle marksmanship, but they require the utmost in accuracy for meaningful results. A paintball is normally .68 caliber or 0.680 inches. For real entertainment, place some on golf tees, back up 50 paces, and try sniping them from prone. It's a great bipod drill that translates well to long-range centerfire work. The trouble is, unless your rifle has the prerequisite accuracy, you'll miss most of them no matter how hard you try. The chart above illustrates the importance of that extra half-inch. If your rifle just can't provide the accuracy required for this drill, you can always move closer. The same paintball array at 40 yards is still challenging enough. No matter what, the odds for good results are slim without some research.

ACCURACY ASSESSMENT

We're talking about the true capability of your rifle, rather than your individual ability. A setup for serious rifle testing requires some thought and planning. In our experience, many shooters don't fully understand the sighting-in process, let alone well-grounded bench rest techniques. The good news is that none of it is rocket science. Real accuracy testing involves elimination of the human elements and any other forces which contribute to erode potential results. Laying a rifle across the hood of a truck might work in a pinch for a makeshift zero check, but it simply won't suffice for serious results. A combination of the right equipment and well-grounded techniques is necessary. This may take some time to perfect, but the experience gained will transfer nicely to other disciplines.

Bench-rest accuracy testing in progress. The long shadows on this range indicate an early morning session – an effort to beat the wind.

Eliminate the variables: Essential items include a solid bench and a good rest. We use a heavy bench-rest tripod with an adjustable sandbag cradle. A second rear bag provides overall stability necessary for optimum results. Comfort is essential for proper and consistent positioning. It takes a while to develop a routine, and organization is necessary to exploit available time. We watch many shooters rush their shots. Add poor positioning, and the results downrange won't be very encouraging. Everything needs to be right, and that includes the wind, or lack thereof. I won't test in conditions other than still air, because results will be degraded. I watch the forecasts and plan for early morning or evening range periods. Ideal conditions include a light overcast, 50-degree temperature and dead calm air. The variables also include range. The bench should be located at a consistent distance!

Targets: I prefer a white background with targets that are black square outlines. Size depends on magnification, but those measuring 1 ½ inches work well. Bullet holes are easily visible, and the crosshairs neatly bisect the targets. You can make a template from a strip of cardboard and trace cutouts with a marking pen to draw squares. A large white-sided IPSC target provides room for lots of squares. All shooting occurs with scopes parallax-corrected for the shooting distance, set on a consistent magnification. Any setting of 6X or more will work at 50 yards. Without a decent scope, don't bother. I will test iron sighted rifles, but the range will decrease to 25 yards. That distance works with dot sights, too. The targets will be black bullseyes.

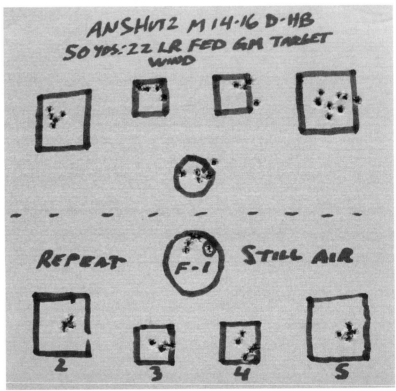

The effects of wind are evident in these series of 50-yard .22 LR groups fired on two different days. The "F-1" indicates the first (or fouling) shot from a clean barrel.

Fouling effects: On hand is a GI ammo can that is filled with an assortment of .22 brands. It's part of a kit that includes targets, a stapler, and marking pens. Everything is organized to capitalize on those brief windows when conditions are right. When switching to a different load, I always fire *at least* five fouling shots. The first few shots are often inconsistent and it sometimes takes a few before accuracy stabilizes. Sometimes, the first shot can be inches off the mark. The second and third shot may begin to settle down, striking closer. Now and then, two or three 5-shot groups may be required before consistent groups develop. The whole process can be very weird. In my experience, the ammunition most likely to produce this effect is match grade stuff, with wax-coated plain lead bullets. Maybe the stiff lubricant requires a few passes through the barrel for consistent influence on accuracy. Plated bullets seem less likely to display such behavior. For example, I can usually depend on 37 grain

Winchester "Super-X" hollow-point .22 LR bullets to fly true from the first shot. I wouldn't use it in a bench rest competition, but it does seem to be a dependable small game load.

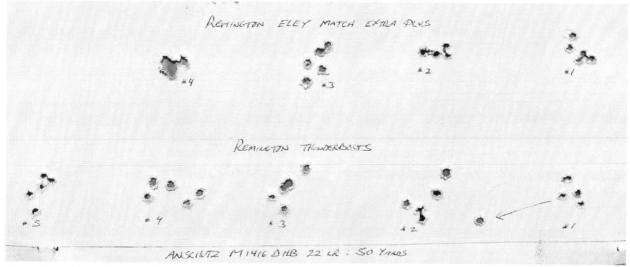

Sometimes it's easier to evaluate groups by reversing a target. The Eley match load is more accurate than the plinker-grade Remington Thunderbolts, which comes as no surprise. Look carefully and you can see groups shrink from both brands as shooting progresses.

Protocols: As I said, iron and dot-sighted .22s can be tested at 25 yards. Neither is ultra-precise, but you can still get a handle on what works the best. Afterwards, back up to 50 yards and shoot some more. Try a few close-range shots at 10 and 15 yards as well. You can then determine your preferred zero.

Scoped rifles chambered for .22 LR are normally zeroed and tested at 50 yards. Later, you can do some mad science with .22 Shorts and CB Caps at closer range. At some point, try the most promising .22 LR loads at 100 yards. You'll likely see why 50 yards makes a good all-around zero.

The .22 WMRs and .17 HMRs should really be evaluated at 100 yards. For either caliber, this is also a practical zero distance. Later, you can shoot at both closer and further ranges to get a handle on trajectory.

I like to fire a series of five 5-shot groups, which progress systematically from left to right. Each group series is recorded on the target with a marking pen. A digital camera is used to capture the data so it can be transferred to the home computer for future reference. If your target paper contains a large amount of groups, it's sometimes helpful to flip it over for viewing from the rear. Without the clutter of circles or data, results are clearly visible.

Resist the temptation to quit shooting if you record a really good group. There is a very good chance it will be a fluke. Some writers throw out their worst shots when calculating group size. Unless you know you pulled one, count every hole. It's not uncommon to see four decent groups and one that isn't pretty. This same effect may occur in reverse. That is why a full five groups are a more reliable indicator of a rifle's real potential. If the wind comes up, it will have an effect, skewing your results. You can either quit or keep shooting, noting the conditions on the target. It's educational to leave the barrel fouled with the same load and reshoot another series in dead calm air. Compare the targets and, with an accurate rifle and load, you'll probably see the effects of wind. You may also note a slight shift in impact points between targets. This may be attributable to other factors like light, temperature, or rest technique.

The dividends: If this seems like a huge amount of effort, well, it is. But don't forget; shooting is fun and you'll get plenty of it. Along the way, you can also refine your technique, which will pay dividends later. I've had the opportunity to fire many thousands of rounds, but I still consciously work on the finer points of marksmanship. I really work on trigger squeeze. My full attention is on the crosshairs: before, during, and after each shot. Follow-through is a very big deal, and when everything works in harmony, some very nice groups are possible. Down the road, when hunkered behind a centerfire marvel of tactical precision, your rimfire experience may pay major dividends. That premium box of .308 will set you back $1.50 per

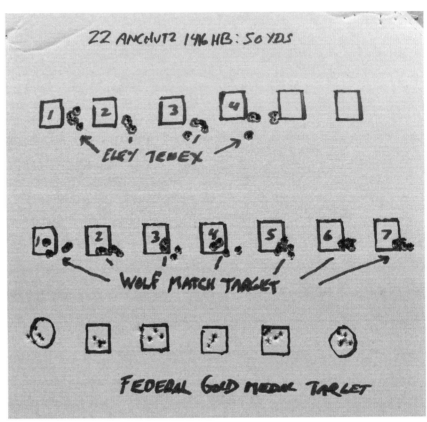

You never know until you try. In this case a couple of in-between .22 LR target loads beat out the highly regarded Eley Tenex match cartridge .

shot. It's reassuring to know your skills have been refined, to help place it where it needs to go.

Back to that iron sighted Marlin Model 60; I really have no idea what its true accuracy potential is. I've never tested it beyond 25 yards. The thumbnail-sized groups it fires there with iron sights are perfectly adequate for its intended use. Shooting is close, fast, and furious - the polar opposite of those detail-oriented efforts involving sandbags.

CHAPTER 10

TRAINING TIPS

I've put some extra work into the rimfire section, mainly because it will serve as a foundation for future rifle coverage. Beyond firearm types, ammunition and accessories, a real gold mine exists for skill development. In case you've been living in another galaxy, ammo prices are through the roof. You could work on shooting positions with centerfire rifle ammo, but you'd better have deep pockets. Price per shot can run around $1.50! I will say this: you'll probably concentrate. Then again, a can will probably hop off a log when hit with a .22 Long Rifle. By using your carefully-selected and similar rimfire rifle, meaningful practice is possible. Besides saving money, you'll be less likely to develop a nasty flinch induced by muzzle blast and recoil. There's no sense in paying extra for bad habits.

BASIC DRILLS

An extremely beneficial tool in our arsenal of tricks is dry-fire practice, during which sight alignment and trigger control are practiced with an unloaded firearm. Concentrating on a sight picture, it's easy to see if it remains undisturbed when the gun goes "click". If properly executed, everything should stay put. We have our new shooters dry-fire up a storm during basic firearms training with center-fire pistols, AR-15 rifles, or pump-action shotguns. However, due to the ignition system of a rimfire, this practice can cause some damage. Without a brass cartridge rim to cushion the blow, a firing pin may contact the edge of a chamber. Eventually, an indent may develop that could burr the chamber edge or cause misfires. Unless you have a rimfire designed for safe dry-firing, the practice should be avoided. Fortunately, a .22 is mild enough to promote good shooting habits using live ammo. The following drills are not only fun, but relevant to ALL rifle shooting.

First, run the rifle on your shoulder! This is a no-brainer with a semi-auto, but many shooters will dismount other actions between shots. Instead, work on cycling it while maintaining a gun mount. This process will require some initial concentration, especially with a bolt-action rifle. It's a wise investment, since time spent here will program you for an inevitable and necessary fast follow-up shot.

Off-hand practice: Pre-zero your rifle for 50 yards. Pick a target roughly four inches in diameter and move forward to 25 yards. Your object is to make five straight hits. You can begin with carefully fired single targets, working on marksmanship fundamentals. Once you have things sorted out, try shooting efficient pairs. Maintain that gun mount in between, and increase your shot count and cadence.

Keep backing up until you can reliably make hits at 50 yards. "Reliably" may not constitute 100% hits, but should involve the majority. A ratio of 80% is reasonable. Those using iron sights will have a tougher time, and dot sight shooters may face challenges resulting from its size. A 6 MOA dot will subtend 3 inches at 50 yards, and nearly cover a 4-inch target. You can always adjust its size or your range to compensate. Scope shooters should stay put at 50 yards, working on technique. Reliably hit 4-inch targets will translate to 8-inch groups at 100 yards, a realistic centerfire expectation.

I have the luxury of a falling plate rack, with 6 resettable four-inch steel disks. More portable rimfire-scaled dueling trees work very well, and offer an opportunity for competition among two shooters. Commercial targets are nice, but you can substitute small paper plates, can bottoms, or even clay pigeons. Anything reactive will save a lot of walking.

A rimfire-sized falling plate rack with knock-down 4" steel disks. A tug on a cord resets the whole array.

Another worthwhile way to save mileage is to move in close, engaging small targets at seven to fifteen yards. With optics, this can be harder than you'd think. The center of a scope is higher than your bore, so offset must be factored in. Draw a few dime-sized spots on a backwards target, and you can see the needed allowance. A head shot minimizes meat damage, and this skill may prove useful on sitting game like grouse or rabbits.

Supported field positions: I'll admit to being a mediocre offhand shooter. Give me a tree or fencepost to brace against and that will change for the better. Support-hand contact really helps, and the addition of strong-side elbow contact is nearly rock steady. Play around with a tree, telephone pole, building edge, or even the corner of a vehicle. Make sure you don't shoot your truck, and allow for unobstructed ejection. Those tricky 50-yard targets should be much more hittable. You can also begin playing with a sling to improve stability. I don't use one often for this purpose, but it's a handy skill to develop.

The outdoor channels often run African safari footage involving shooting sticks. These may be just a pair of simple connected stakes, or more elaborate commercial telescoping legs similar to a camera tripod. Single, dual, or three-legged versions are available to help create a stable shooting platform. As often as not, a guide will be carrying the sticks while the hunter manages the rifle. I don't use shooting sticks often, but concede that they do have value. A rimfire rifle is a great way to become comfortable with them, too. I prefer a two-legged version, connecting the rifle's forend against the bipod top with a firm support hand grip. Precise elevation adjustments can be made by angling the legs. If you need less height, just back up a bit, rocking the sticks until things feel right. Accuracy is greatly improved when this standing technique is mastered. It takes a while to telescope the legs to your individual height, something you can play around with using a .22 rifle. After standing shots are mastered, you can shorten the legs and try some kneeling or sitting shots. Results should be surprisingly good!

Next, ditch the support and work on more kneeling and sitting shots. For many folks, these positions will be much more stable than any unsupported offhand attempts. Often, terrain, vegetation, or time will preclude their use, but sitting and kneeling positions are still worth mastering.

Prone stage of fire during a rifle qualification course.

The last stop is prone. I'll go this route any time I can, and it's a common position on military and law enforcement qualification courses. However, the same limiting factors of time and terrain are even more pronounced from prone. Essentially, you'll be lying on your belly, low to the ground, using two braced elbows to eliminate most human tremors. A proper prone position is amazingly accurate, but can present surprises for shooters using some action types. Pump guns become much more difficult to cycle, especially in centerfire stroke lengths. Lever-actions require position shifts, and barrel-cocking airguns are a real challenge. Your scope's eye relief may suddenly become too short as well. Again, a rimfire rifle offers a great means to work through these issues, especially if it is similar to your centerfire choice. For the ultimate field stability, attach a bipod. We'll cover this accessory during precision shooting drills.

ADVANCED DRILLS

Once the basics are mastered, you may want to add a few skill sets. Especially when framed in the context of centerfire rifle use, it's reassuring to be able to function in unexpected situations.

Support-side (or weak-side) shooting: For many of us, this means we'll be shooting left-handed. A .22 is a perfect trainer, since you won't rock yourself into the next county with a poorly delivered shot. It's a handy skill as well. I've shot two deer left-handed, including one during 2011. Sometimes it's hard to get turned around, and in this case, the extra movement would've cost me the deer. Defensively, we consider ambidextrous operation important. Not only could you lose a hand, but you could also sustain a dominant eye injury. Particularly with the extreme sight height of an AR-15, it's easier than you might think to blast a bullet into cover. Any hard surface will deflect particles or bullet fragments at eye level. The same holds true for incoming fire. It's worth learning how to swap hands - not only for shooting, but also for loading and operation.

Speed-shooting: Even the best optical systems have limitations imposed by light and weather. So sometimes, just a good gun mount will have to do. With proper fitting, if your eye is right above the barrel, you'll probably shoot somewhere near to where you're looking. That's the principle of effective shotgun wing-shooting, and the same theory can be applied for close and fast rifle work. This drill is geared for iron sights. A semi-auto is just the ticket, but an AR clone won't work.

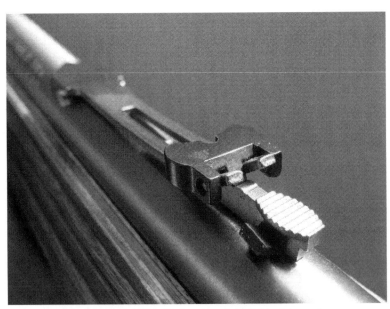

Marlin Model 60 with its rear sight folded down for ultra-fast close-quarter shooting.

Start with a large target at fairly close range. I like an IDPA combat silhouette, which has an inner scoring circle, but a paper plate will work. I bought my Marlin Model 60 because of its folding rear sight blade. With it down, mount and fire as soon as the stock hits your cheek, referencing strictly off your front sight. If you have a shot timer, set it for 2 seconds and shoot from only 10 paces. With an okay gun fit, you'll probably see a group develop. Keep at it and incrementally reduce the par time until you're making hits within 1 second. With practice, you'll become fast and surprisingly accurate. You can back up, switch to cans, or better yet, shift to multiple targets. This presents an opportunity to work on another rapid-fire skill: sear reset (also known as prepping the trigger). After breaking a shot, hold the trigger fully rearward, pause and ease it forward just to the point where you can feel a click. Then squeeze shot two. Using multiple targets, you can start with a pair, engaging the first while working on sear reset as you transition to the second. Eventually, you can expand your array, which is why I like our 6-plate rack. When harmony is achieved the plates can be quickly flattened while maintaining a noticeably smooth sense of control.

On smallish targets, you might want to start with a complete front/rear sight picture, but don't be afraid to eventually ditch that rear sight. You'll probably shoot high if you just look over it, which is why I like a folding rear blade. Once you know where your bullets are hitting, it's time for moving targets like balls or ground-rolled fruit. Aerial targets are a hoot, but extremely dangerous without a safe bullet drop zone. We've been known to shoot at quartering incoming clay birds, using our remote control machines. It's tricky but doable, and it all boils down to practice. Remember that .22 bullets can travel more than a mile.

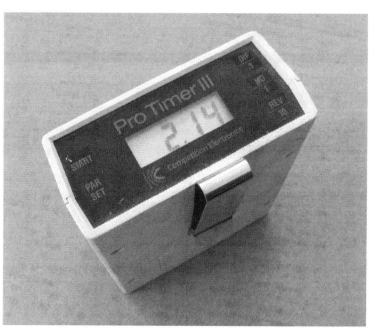

A shot timer makes a great training tool. This display indicates delivery of a shot 2.14 seconds after a start tone. Multiple reports can be recorded along with the intervals between them.

I'd plan on burning lots of ammo. A tubular magazine works great. The pre-filled Spee-D-Loaders keep the action rolling, and the inexpensive ammo keeps a lid on costs. Fun? You bet!

Precision shooting: It seems as though long-range shooting is all the rage these days. The market abounds with rifles, scopes, and gear specifically designed to permit accurate shooting on the far side of a quarter mile. A folding, rifle-mounted bipod is a key piece of the puzzle, providing near bench rest stability from prone field positions. The firearm will probably be a bolt-action rifle or tricked-out semi-auto like an AR-15. As such, the comments that follow apply mainly to users of such action types. There often isn't any *practical* way to attach a bipod to other systems. There are inexpensive, spring-loaded bipods that clamp to a barrel like a clothespin. Since you really don't want to put any pressure (or hard contact point) on your barrel, save your money. A bipod that hooks on to a rifle's forend is much better. If the barrel is free-floated in the stock, clearance will allow some upward pressure without a corresponding change of zero.

The flip-side of speed-shooting: A Harris Bipod mounted to a free-float AR-15 forend. The legs adjust for height and can be folded.

As for bipods, I'm a Harris Bipod fan, having used them for decades. Nowadays, several clones are sold for less money. They can be easily attached to the front QD sling swivel stud of a rifle's forend using a thumb screw. The legs stow parallel to the barrel, but pivot 90 degrees downward, proving solid support when properly adjusted. With practice and the right type, you can get into a useful position very quickly.

The key is practice. At first, you may encounter difficulties putting everything together. It'll take a while to figure out the right leg height adjustments, which may vary depending on terrain and elevation. For me, the Harris 9-to-13" model works best. Folding the legs down provides the 9-inch height, but I normally need more. Release tabs permit the telescoping inner sections to extend until things seem right. Because I seldom use its full extension, the Harris notched-leg model comes in handy. A click stop engages each notch in graduated intervals, for consistent leg lengths. On uneven terrain, the swivel head model will allow rotation of the rifle until the crosshairs are level. I still have a basic Harris with friction-lock legs and a non-swiveling head. Infinite adjustments are possible through the use of thumb screws that secure the leg extensions. It's a bit more uncomfortable to set up from prone though. With either type, once the right height is figured out it's often easier to adjust the legs in standing, while the bipod is still folded forward. You can extend each leg the same amount by eyeballing their relative positions.

Lining up on a woodchuck with a Ruger .17 HMR, prone off a bipod.

A couple of other issues involve eye relief and stock cheek-weld. In prone the scope may seem too far rearward unless this factor is considered during the mechanical mounting process. With a low-recoil rifle it's just aggravating but, a hard-kicking centerfire could drive the ocular bell into your orbital socket. A good place to figure this out is during controlled conditions with your rimfire! As for cheek weld, solid contact helps. You may experience the sensation of a floating head, which can degrade overall stability and cause difficulties maintaining a full scope image. I prefer to shoot with my elbows under the rifle and my upper body elevated a bit. True, I'm not as low to the ground, but the more upright position is more in line with a scope set up for other field positions. I put some forward but consistent pressure on both bipod legs, and hook my support arm below the stock near my strong-side armpit. Once everything is properly locked in, a very stable platform will result. You'll still see a small amount of crosshair movement, but it won't be much. As long as they're wandering inside your target, a hit should be possible with gradual trigger squeeze. Again, an accurate .22 rifle is a great tool for development of a personalized techniques that can transfer effectively (along with your bipod) to long-range centerfire rifles.

The .22 LR Anschutz works similarly to the.223 Remington M-700,
providing a great opportunity for scaled-down practice.

Scaled-down targets work at shorter ranges. These .680" paintballs are set at 50 yards.
They need a dab of glue to stay put in wind.

There's something satisfying about whacking a gong or rock several football fields away. However, for many of us, limiting factors involve both financial resources and a practical location. What to do? How about scaling things down? A carefully chosen .22 LR, with a similar manual of arms, can be used at greater distances than many folks realize. We'll often shoot 100-yard golf balls from a prone field position, using an agency .308 off a bipod. Switching to paintballs on golf tees at 50 yards will provide a similar challenge if your .22 can maintain 1/2" groups (1 MOA). I tried saltine crackers at 100 yards, which were fairly easy, but not too spectacular (they just showed a hole instead of breaking). Fired shotgun shells at 50 yards are fun, as are empty 9mm cases at 25 yards. You get the idea. Just plop down in prone, extend your bipod legs and have some fun.

Improvised targets: Saltine crackers doubled as 100-yard targets and snack-food. One problem with edible targets is that they often get eaten.

Just for grins, I shot some 200-yard groups with my .22 LR bolt-action Anschutz 1416 HB. I used Federal Gold Medal Target ammo off a shooting bench. From extensive testing, I knew this load would average half-inch, five-shot groups at 50 yards in still air. The Burris 4x12 scope has target turrets that permit easy adjustments for various ranges, within reason. But, 200 yards is really a stretch, so I researched the drop and positioned a higher aiming point. I also waited for dead calm conditions. Firing carefully, the result was a series of two-inch, five-shot groups that printed around five feet low. I could see the bullets in flight as they lobbed in, and it was loads of fun.

SUMMARY

An accurate .22 rifle provides opportunities for some interesting shooting beyond basic plinking. Sound techniques can be refined for much less cost, compared to centerfire practice. Due to lower velocity and longer bore-time, follow-through is essential. I place all my focus on those crosshairs before, during, and after each shot. The slightest glitch will be aggravatingly evident, but will hone your rifle ability in all areas.

A two-inch group fired with .22 LR Federal Gold Medal Target (visible on bottom of center target) at 200 yards. The Anschutz M-1516 D-HB was zeroed at 50 yards and the aiming point was the circle in the upper target!

These inexpensive spring-loaded steel Champion targets re-set automatically. They come with ground stakes but this array was screwed down. Hits can be erased with spray paint.

Target sources: Your grocery store will work for Necco wafers, lollipops, and food dyes that can turn ice cubes into neat reactive targets. Some entertaining commercial products are made by Do-All and Champion. Birchwood Casey's Shoot-N-C targets are popular adhesives that display highly visible hits. Besides your local gun shop, they can be sourced through Cabela's, Graf & Sons, Midway USA, Brownell's, Natchez, and even Wally World.

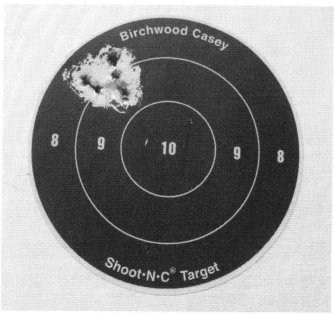

Birchwood Casey's adhesive "Shoot-N-C" targets clearly indicate your hits.

CHAPTER 11

USEFUL LOADS

What follows are a few good loads that have performed consistently, both for me and some trusted acquaintances. This is only anecdotal evidence. No doubt many shooters will have opposite experiences. The list is intentionally short and covers only those loads we've had the best results with, in a large sampling of rifles, over relatively long periods of time. You won't see the 5mm Remington or .17 Mach 2, because I don't have sufficient experience to draw from.

.22 LONG RIFLE AMMUNITION

To gain the best possible accuracy, you'll probably need premium match ammunition from companies like Eley or Lapua, which will cost at least three times as much as standard loads. From a top-flight target rifle, you may see true ½ MOA groups or better.

Mass-produced, lower cost .22 ammo shoots reasonably well, all things considered. Still, it's hard to get consistently tight groups. Just when things start looking encouraging, fliers appear and groups expand. Some fanatics resort to sorting individual cartridges by weight and rim thickness. Others occasionally luck out and stumble upon a fairly consistent rifle and ammo combination capable of approaching match load accuracy. Although I've had no such miracles, I have discovered a few reliable performers.

The assortment of useful loads covered below.

Federal Gold Medal Target, 40 grain lead round-nose #711B: This is Federal's lower-priced match load, and I've had good luck with it in many rifles. It shouldn't be confused with Premium Match, which costs more than twice as much. You can buy Gold Medal Target two ways: either as a standard-velocity version rated at 1080 fps, or a high-velocity 1200 fps type. I haven't tried the HV load, but I had enough confidence in the slower flavor to buy a 5,000 round case. The only rifle that's been a bust so far was a Ruger/Volquartsen custom 10/22. It shot everything else, so the reason remains a mystery. I swapped its barrel out for a second VQ, and immediately had a tack driver. Such is the nature of .22 rifle and ammo combinations. I mainly shoot this GMT load at inanimate targets. It groups well in many pistols or rifles, and I zero the latter at 50 yards. It has just enough power to run most semi-autos, and accuracy can approach MOA in good barrels.

Remington Subsonic Hollow-Point, 38 grain Lead #SUB22HP: In my experience, this load is a bit less accurate than Federal's GMT, but makes a more humane choice for small game hunting. Velocity is listed at 1050 fps and I shoot it interchangeably, using the same GMT 50-yard zero. At 25 yards, either load will strike only a hair higher for spot-on aiming. The Subsonic is a better squirrel load. Accuracy is more than adequate in most rifles - it doesn't damage much meat. It's also very quiet in rifles. I'll often sit in one spot with a scoped bolt-action and take several squirrels without shaking things up. Considering its mild nature, I'm surprised it runs reliably through most semi-auto rifles. My custom 10/22 eats it right up, but some pistol-shooters report function problems.

Effect of Remington .22 LR "Subsonic" HP on squirrels, using a Remington M-504. The results are humane but meat damage isn't excessive.

Winchester Super-X Hollow-Point High Velocity, 37 grain #X22LRH: This load is another rung up the power ladder. I always keep a couple 500-round bricks on hand for general rimfire duties. Velocity is rated at 1280 fps and accuracy, so far, has been consistently good. It costs just a bit more than bulk pack loads, but offers no surprises. I've seen a number of 50-yard, 5-shot groups that ran around 5/8" and ¾" is not uncommon. Groups, if not superb, are surprisingly consistent, with no wide fliers. Because velocity is similar to other offerings, major sight adjustments aren't necessary. It's not a fussy load, and always seems to cut predictable groups without any fouling shots. The bullets are copper-plated, which seems to minimize gunk. I don't see misfires, and feeding is completely reliable. Performance on game is fine as well. What more could we ask for?

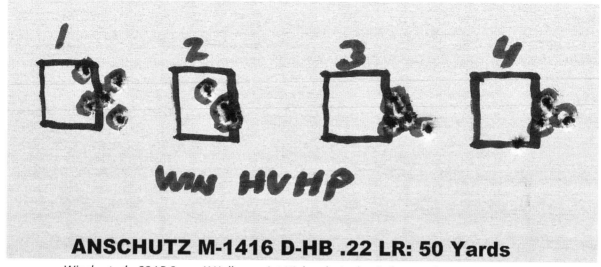

Winchester's .22 LR Super-X Hollow-point High-velocity load often produces good accuracy, making it a viable all-around choice for many rifles.

CCI Velocitor Copper-Plated Hollow-Point, 40 grain #0047: For anyone looking to increase the punch of their .22 rifle, CCI's aptly-named Velocitors are worth a look. Muzzle velocity is listed at 1435 fps – a significant gain over conventional high-speed choices (which typically rely on lighter bullets to help boost performance). CCI has a trajectory chart based on a 75-yard zero. At 50 yards, rounds strike 0.9" high. They drop 2.5" at 100 yards, which is quite an improvement. I've seen consistently good 50-yard accuracy in a number of rifles, all of which

Two hot CCI loads: Note the Stinger's longer cartridge case.

averaged under 0.75 inch. When switching from normal high-speeds, you will need a zero change, since the extra velocity results in higher strikes. For larger animals like woodchucks, though, the effort is worth the time. This performance comes at additional cost that keeps the Velocitor off a plinking list. While the .22 Long Rifle really isn't a true defensive cartridge, out of all loads commonly available, this one might be the best bet. The Velocitor manages to wring out an extra 150 fps with a full-weight projectile.

CCI Stinger Hyper Velocity Copper-Plated Hollow-Point, 32 grain #0050: Here's the load that started the hyper-speed craze. The "Stinger" achieves maximum speed thanks to a lighter bullet, longer case, and improved propellant. Its light bullet leaves a rifle barrel at 1640 fps, which is screaming fast for a .22 Long Rifle. Without a zero change, groups will impact significantly higher. Despite claims to the contrary, I've seen surprisingly good accuracy with Stingers. However, unlike everything else listed so far, it's far from guaranteed. If fortune smiles and good groups form at 50 paces, try backing up to 100 yards. You may or may not see correspondingly good results. In the event that you do, compare the drop against standard high-speeds. If both loads are sighted in for 50 yards, you'll see noticeably less drop with Stingers. The lighter bullets will readily expand to damage meat. But, on thin-skinned varmints at further distances, they work well. I've seen 50-yard groups in the 5/8" range from a few bolt-action rifles. Some of the hypervelocity loads have a reputation for erratic accuracy, but you never really know until you try them. Results may run from really bad to surprisingly good.

Caution: Avoid tighter match chambers, which could be damaged by the slightly longer case!

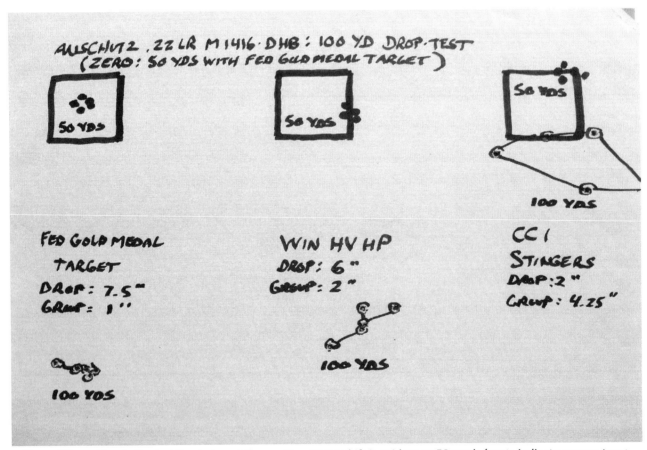

Three different loads fired while aiming at the squares. Some shift is evident at 50 yards (spots indicate groups transposed from a previous target). Note the 100-yard drops and greatly expanded Stinger group.

SPECIALIZED .22 LOADS

CCI .22 CB Long #00038: This quiet load provides the means to turn your .22 rifle into an airgun. The bullet's weight isn't listed on the box, but is probably 29 grains. At roughly 700 fps, it has "Magnum" air rifle punch without more noise. Accuracy, although not spectacular, is adequate for use on pests out to 25 yards. Squirrels should be taken with headshots only. Because the case is LR length, CB Longs will feed through many .22 Long Rifle actions. Unlike a CB Short, it won't leave a fouling ring in the chamber either. A CB Long lacks the force needed to cycle semi-autos, but rounds can be manually fed by racking the charging handle. They're lots of fun to shoot! In a rifle, the report is nil. In a handgun, it's much more noticeable.

CCI .22 Target Short #0037: You can buy high-speed shorts but I prefer the standard-velocity types, using them to increase power above a CB Cap. Bullet weight remains 29 grains, but velocity increases roughly 250 fps. If you can't find CB Caps, this load will stand in nicely. It's nearly as quiet, and reach is increased. I sometimes shoot them from 25 to 50 yards, using my old Remington M-510 single-shot bolt-action rifle. The 24" barrel minimizes noise while producing a muzzle velocity of 950 fps. Accuracy is surprisingly good at 25 yards.

Drawbacks: They may not feed well through many .22 LR actions, due to their short overall length. You'll also need to brush out the chamber or a ring of fouling will develop. This can impede feeding and ejection of .22 LR rounds. The latter situation could also result in a live round not being extracted. Be sure to check!

A common zero and aiming point illustrate the effects of bullet weight and velocity on the trajectories of .22 LR (1080 fps); .22 Short (950 fps); and .22 CB Caps (675 fps). Each load was fired at 50 and 25 yards. The default zero was 50 yards, using a Federal .22 LR Gold Medal Target load.

Tip: By zeroing first at 50 yards with .22 Federal Gold Medal Target, the CCI Target Shorts are on at 25 yards. CBs hit around an inch low. The mild velocity of the .22 Long Rifle target load makes this possible.

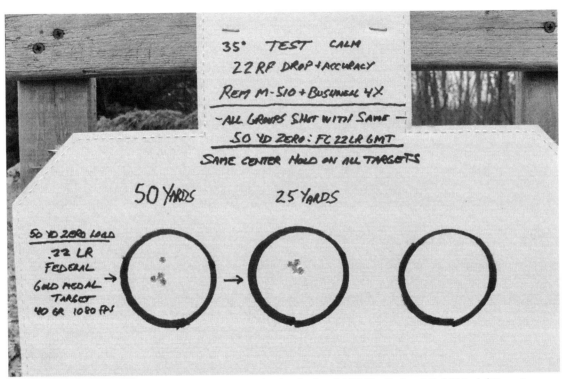

A 50-yard zero works well, even with standard-velocity .22 LR like Federal Gold Medal Target.

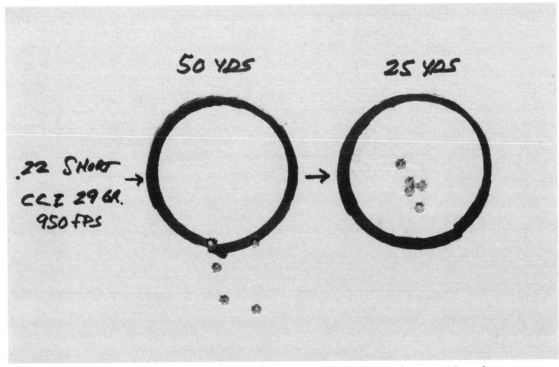

The same 50-yard zero used with .22 LR also worked with 22 Shorts at 25 yards.
Outside circle diameters are 3-inches.

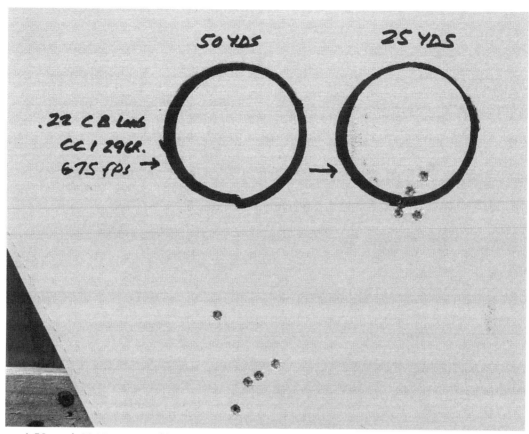

A 50-yard .22 LR zero would work with CB Caps at 25 yards by holding on the top edge of the 3-inch circle, or roughly 1 ½" high.

The targets in this series were shot using a very basic rifle and scope. Note the chronograph 15 feet down range.

CCI .22 Long Rifle Shotshell #0039: A .22 shot cartridge is a real niche load. I always maintain a small stash, which lasts a very long time. Forget any meaningful wing-shooting practice due to the tiny shot payload. But for close-range snakes or rats in the chicken coop, it might be just the ticket.

Velocities were recorded by shooting test loads over a chronograph. This particular shot is a Federal .22 LR Gold Medal Target, which clocked 1078 feet-per-second.

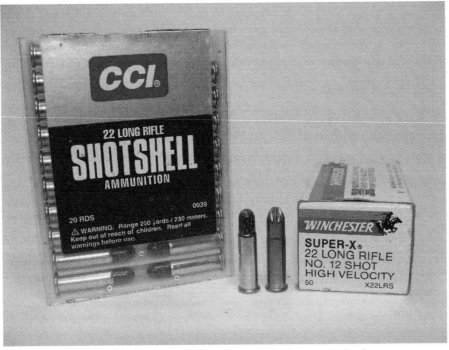

Two types of .22 LR shot cartridges, both of which are strictly close-range propositions.

Winchester Super-X .22 Long Rifle No. 12 Shot High Velocity #22LRS: Same comments as above. Buy what you can find. Consider feeding, too. Neither load will likely run a semi-auto, and may prove problematic in other actions. You can usually single-load them, though. My Marlin M-39 lever-action does feed the crimped Winchester load, which leads to a story…

I once left a walk-through basement door open while doing some outdoor chores. Later, I was shocked to discover a bobwhite quail under my reloading bench. Further exploration revealed a second one, both of which were very much alive. They were apparently escapees from a game bird farm located a mile up the road. With the concerted efforts of my Labrador, it still took nearly an hour to catch the first quail. I carefully carried it to the backyard and let it go, whereupon it banged a 180 degree turn and flew right back in the basement. After the better part of a second hour, I shifted to plan B, shut the door, and gave things 24 hours to settle down. The quail appeared more comfortable and began touring the cel-

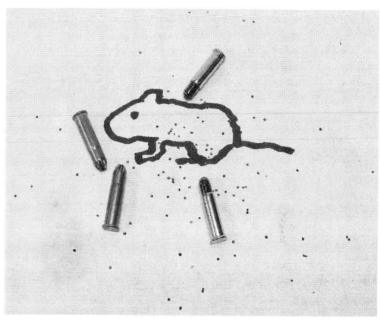

This life-sized mouse target was shot at 15 feet with a crimped Winchester .22 LR "rat shot" cartridge, using a Marlin M-39 with Micro-Groove rifling.

lar. When one landed on the push handle of a lawnmower, I let him have it with a dose of #12 shot. His buddy flew some laps, but my Marlin Model 39 finally laid him low. So far, I'm the only guy I know who has gone quail hunting in his basement.

Rimfire shot-shells are pathetically anemic, but they do have their place. Collateral damage was minimal and the quail were edible. CCI's plastic capsule version is also available in .22 WMR. I'm not sure one is a whole lot better than the other, given their tiny payload.

.22 MAGNUM WINCHESTER RIMFIRE

It's been a while since I played with a .22 WMR, and the number of interesting loads has since increased. A friend in Florida has recently focused on the lighter, faster loads like CCI's 30 grain offering. Still, it's reassuring to know that an old standby is still available.

Winchester Super-X Jacketed Hollow-Point, 40 grain #X22MH: Like me, this load has been around for many years. As such, we have some history. It's just a matter of time until another .22 Magnum crosses my path, and this will be the first load I'll reach for. Extensive testing may reveal a better choice in an individual rifle, but I'll expect this load to shoot decently. At 1910 fps, within reasonable distances to 100 yards or further, effective terminal results are likely. I never found it lacking on woodchucks or porcupines. The Super-X load also functions well in repeating rifles, including semi-automatics. In two different Ruger Model 77/22s, groups ran right at one MOA. In fact, accuracy was fairly close to that in every rifle I tried.

A trusted friend enjoys good results with these .22 WMR loads.

Hornady V-Max, 30 grain (polymer-tipped bullet) #83202: A trusted friend has achieved excellent accuracy with this load in several rifles, and semi-auto function has been positive as well. At 2200 fps, velocity is higher due to the lighter bullet. This increase should flatten trajectory and produce more explosive results on prairie dog-sized varmints. For edible game or larger animals, the Winchester 40 grain load would be the better choice. Don't shoot the 30 grainers in a Magnum Research .22 WMR rifle.

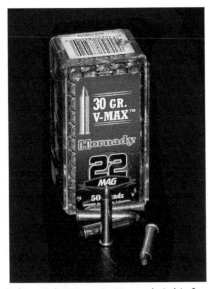

The lightweight 30-grain Hornady is his favorite.

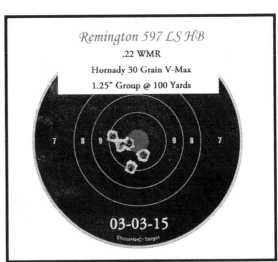

Hornady's .22 WMR 30-grain "V-Max" made a good 100-yard showing on this handy "Shoot-N-C" target. The rifle was Remington's laminated-stock M-597 semi-auto.

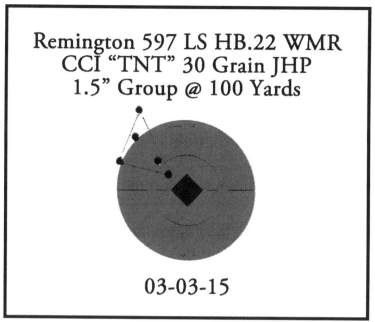

Remington 597 LS HB.22 WMR
CCI "TNT" 30 Grain JHP
1.5" Group @ 100 Yards

03-03-15

CCI's .22 WMR 30-grain TNT wasn't far behind. It usually boils down to hitting the magic combination by trial and error.

CCI's .22 WMR 30-grain TNT, another good high-velocity choice.

.17 HORNADY MAGNUM RIMFIRE

The lone box of .22 WMR gathering dust on a nearby shelf is doing so because of this newfangled rimfire. As I've said, in the woods or on larger game, the .22 Magnum is probably a better pick. But, since other calibers are also on hand here, the .17 HMR has become my number one varmint choice in settled areas. The guys that started it all have their name on the box.

This chunky woodchuck was no match for Hornady's .17 HMR, despite its tiny 17-grain bullet. It makes a nice choice in settled areas.

Hornady Varmint Express, 17 grain V-Max #83170: For those not inclined to experiment, give this one a try. After running it through a number of rifles, I've never seen anything but good results. You may discover a more accurate load, but the difference will probably be slight. Supposedly, Hornady makes bullets for everyone else, so terminal effectiveness should be constant in similar barrels. I'm not sure why the little bullets are so darned accurate. Possibly, part of the reason (beyond close tolerances) has to do with their tiny diameter. Any defects would be closer to its axis and less likely to affect stability. Whatever, it just shoots. I buy it by the 500-round brick to obtain constant lot numbers. I'm not even sure that matters. One thing's for sure: when that little 17 grain bullet smacks a crow inside 125 yards, the effect resembles electrocution. All the manufacturers list MVs of around 2550 fps. In perfect conditions with dead calm air, accuracy is sub-MOA. I can think of no reason to switch.

SUMMARY

Again, these are just my findings. With so many rifles and so many loads, the choices are nearly endless. As I've said, rimfires – particularly .22s - can be ultra-finicky. The best way to find out what shoots in your rifle is to head for the range. My favorite loads may prove disastrous in your firearms. If you track down a winner, stock up on ammo. Look for the same lot numbers and store your supply in a cool, dry place. GI ammo cans work well for this.

Ammo sources: As of this writing in early 2015, rimfire ammunition – particularly .22 types - remains extremely scarce. When we do stumble onto some, customer purchase limits aren't uncommon. I always check the ammo case at Wal-Mart. More often than not it's empty, but some may appear at times. Your local firearms dealer may also luck into a stash. You can also mail-order ammunition. Gander Mountain emails a weekly ammunition alert. Graf & Sons lists in-stock brands first. Midway USA, Brownell's, and Cabela's are always worth checking.

CHAPTER 12

ACCESSORIES

One nice thing about owning a rimfire – especially a .22 – is its simplicity. You probably won't need a rangefinder, wind meter, or thousand dollar scope. Assuming you've already chosen a sighting system, here's a short list broken into two categories:

ESSENTIALS

This list is both short and affordable. However, one significant expense not shown is a sighting system. The personal choice may elevate your system cost substantially. Get through that, and you're almost home free.

Sling: I keep a few on hand with quick-disconnect swivels. If your rifles have QD studs, you can transfer a sling as needed in just a few seconds. One place I often use one is in the woods when squirrel hunting. A compact set of good binoculars helps locate them and the process is a whole lot easier when both hands are available. Once properly adjusted, a sling can also provide greater rifle stability. The shoulder and support arm can be connected through tension for less wobble and greater accuracy. Some slings are fairly elaborate, with large shoulder pads, ammo carriers, and hardware. I'm perfectly happy with a basic nylon model and QD swivels. It'll be quiet, and it can also be easily dried. My favorite is a "mountain sling", which has sewn-in QD swivels, a thin leather lining in the shoulder area, and 1 ¼" width. I'm not sure who made it, however, several similar products can be found on the web. The Blackhawk and Butler Creek products look pretty close, and run around $20 with swivels. When not in use, I just roll them up, securing the coil with an elastic band.

Gun case: A soft zippered version will do. Just make sure it will accommodate whatever optical sight is mounted on your rifle. You should be able to pick one up for $35 or less.

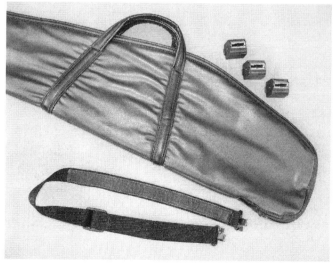

A few essential accessories, including a "mountain" sling with a sewn in non-slip rubber section and QD swivels..

With careful shopping, you can choose one that will also fit your centerfire rifles. For more money, you can buy a hardshell case, affording greater protection and locking capability. About the only time I use a hardshell model is while traveling out of state. The extra protection helps defend against crushing from luggage or gear, and also satisfies locking requirements imposed by some states. For local jaunts, the soft case works fine in my less restrictive area.

Cleaning kit: Every shooter will need one. Fortunately, one basic kit can handle most firearms, as well as .22 caliber airguns (with different lubes). Cost for a prepackaged system isn't prohibitive, and the specifics will be discussed in the "Cleaning" Chapter.

Extra magazines: It's worth having at least one spare. They're usually affordable, so extras are good insurance. Not only can you misplace one, but it may get cantankerous. The first step in solving malfunctions should be a different magazine. It's not a bad idea to mark each one so an offender can be isolated for further investigation. I just use a vibrating pen, engraving an unobtrusive number on each one.

Eye and ear protection: Don't shoot without either. One of the nastiest pressure excursions I saw involved an out-of-battery .22 LR incident. A semi-automatic rifle managed to fire without its bolt fully forward. The cartridge wasn't completely seated, and ruptured upon discharge at the bolt and chamber gap. I pulled a good-sized chunk of brass from my nose and was peppered by other particles. I was just a bystander, too! Fortunately, all parties were wearing shooting glasses, and no one was seriously injured. Bullet pieces can also splatter off hard surfaces, so read any distance warnings for steel targets. Since even a .22's report will degrade your hearing, take appropriate cautions. These measures apply to you, as well as others in your vicinity!

OTHER GOODIES

These are things we don't have to have. Some can be picked up incidentally for use with different guns.

Ammo can: They're handy for long-term ammunition storage. Lead bullets tend to oxidize, so a moisture-proof container helps. The collapsible handle is good for range trips, and folds flat for stacking. Real men use them for lunch boxes.

Spee-D-Loader: For those with tubular-magazine rifles, this quick-fill reservoir is a mighty handy item. I keep mine loaded, so up to 120 rounds are immediately on hand. The clear plastic body indicates its status at a glance. Eight annular com-

A slightly out-of-battery semi-auto discharge caused this result. Hot gas and brass shrapnel were expelled through the breech, making a great case for shooting glasses!

partments each hold up to 15 rounds of .22 LR ammo stacked end to end. A twist cap with a spout can be indexed above each compartment. Line everything up, and you can simply pour a reload into your rifle, parking the cap between compartments afterwards. My Marlin M60 holds 14 rounds, so that's what I load in each compartment. This device is probably too big to lug around, but sure is handy during plinking-fests. It also works with .22 WMR, holding up to 11 rounds per compartment. Cost is about $25. Go to their website and you'll see other sizes listed, including a short 48-round version which might be fairly portable. FYI, the site also lists a carrying pouch for the 120-round device.

Marble Arms Catch .22: This ammo holder should prove useful for anyone, since loose rimfire ammo in a pocket is a bother. Not only can it be difficult to access (especially during winter months), but the lubricated .22 LR types can accumulate dirt and lint. So here's a clever and portable rimfire reservoir in a compact size. Ten staggered vertical compartments inside a compact housing each hold five .22 LR

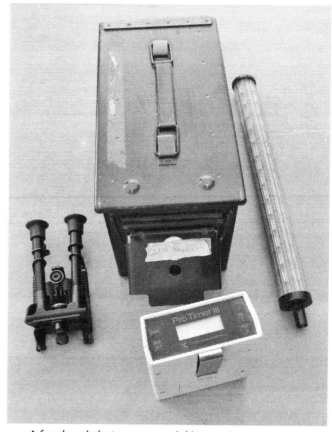

A few handy but non-essential items: G.I. ammo cans hold lots of rimfire ammunition. For those serious about skill development a shot timer is a valuable training aid, as is a bipod.

rounds for a total capacity of 50. The cartridges drop in vertically, and a sliding lid exposes just one compartment at a time. The plastic body has a belt clip, and cost is less than $12. I haven't yet used one, but you can bet I will! Supposedly, this device will also accommodate .22 airgun pellets.

Bipod: The next best thing to a full-blown shooting bench is this two-legged rifle attachment. The most well-known example is a "Harris Bipod", which is available in several configurations. As we discussed in the training Chapter, its base attaches to the QD sling stud on a forearm of a rifle, using a simple tension screw. The base houses two spring-loaded folding legs, which are quick to deploy. Several different heights are offered, and each has telescoping leg sections to permit additional extension with precise adjustments. I don't normally roam afield with a bipod on a .22 rimfire, but it sure makes a great centerfire training aid. As previously explained, hook one on an accurate rifle and you can learn how to master bipod techniques on reduced-scale targets. There are a number of Harris clones for sale, but I don't have any experience with them.

On the other hand, my oldest Harris is still going strong after more than 35 years. My favorite is their HBMLS with 9 -13" notched leg stops and a swivel feature. A less expensive model is sold without the swivel feature and friction-knob leg locks. It's also harder to adjust from prone. The shortest 6-9" model will work for many folks. It's a bit too low for me, making it a bench affair. Mine sees much less use than the all-around 9-13" version. Cost is around $100, but it can be used on a number of different rifles. A bipod may not be for everyone though. If your interest lies with a basic firearms inventory, the collection listed in *Survival Guns* makes some sense. Three Remington pump-action types were shown, including a shotgun, rimfire, and centerfire rifle. They're field-expedient choices, but not well suited for a bipod. Neither is a lever-action, and although it is probably technically possible to mount one, I'd focus more on field positions.

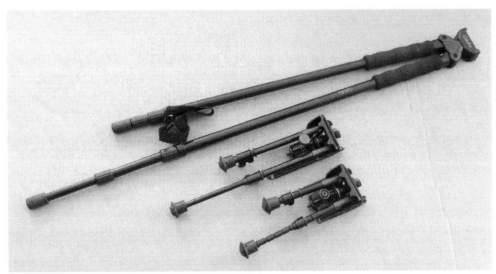

The two-legged shooting stick works from standing or kneeling positions. The Harris Bipods are great prone aids. The 6-9" has notched leg detents and the 9-13" employs friction locks.

This AR-15 is decked out with a number of useful accessories including the shorter 6-9" Harris Bipod that many shooters prefer.

Bench rest tripod and bags: The *next best thing* is a rifle-mounted bipod. But for serious accuracy work, the stability of bench-mounted supports is hard to beat. You can spend several hundred dollars on a top end, fully adjustable, heavy cast tripod with fitted bags. We maintain a Wichita unit on our range, along with several sandbags. It's made from a heavy casting and has pointed, screw-adjustable feet at the end of each low tripod leg. A central threaded stem adjusts to various heights, using a large thumb wheel. A metal cradle on top holds an eared leather sandbag for proper forend support. A separate, larger-eared bag is positioned at the rear of the shooting bench to cradle the rifle's stock. Once properly set up, rock-steady support can be maintained. That takes most of the human equation out of serious accuracy testing. Caldwell sells a similar but more reasonably-priced unit for less than $130. It's called "The Rock Shooting Rest & Rear Bag Combo", which comes range-ready with both bags.

Bench-rest with bags set up for serious accuracy work. This one is a heavy, cast iron Wichita unit.

Light: Like a bipod, this accessory isn't completely necessary. In fact, if I was only going to own one rifle and it was a .22 rimfire, I'd probably skip both items. But in the context of this book series, a rimfire constitutes only part of an overall firearms collection, so at least one centerfire rifle, as well as a handgun, are still in the cards. My bipods jump around a collection of rifles, and my favorite light sees even more diverse use. A Safariland RLS 90-lumen tactical light fills the bill nicely, thanks to its QD mount. Although initially procured for use on a pistol, the Picatinny interface slips handily on to the forend rails of an S&W AR-22 rifle. Voila: an instant anti-critter 'gitter results. I slide mine back near the receiver on the rifle's left side until my support hand thumb can easily contact the light's tail end push button. This combination is also a reassuring bump-in-the-night tool when matched to a 25-round magazine full of .22 hollow-points. The RLS costs less than $100, and I've seen it on sale for much less. By pivoting the light in its mounting housing, a tab engages a Picatinny rail slot. Since many rifles don't have that feature, it's not for everyone.

S&W M&P 15-22 with a Safariland RLS light mounted to a Picatinny rail on its forend.

Shot timer: This accessory is one of those non-essential items that can prove valuable for those seeking to maximize their shooting abilities. The Competition Electronics $110 Pocket Pro 2 is an economical example. It "hears" each shot and displays its time, relative to a start tone. A shooter can either set a random start signal or use an instant button. Afterwards, each shot can be reviewed through a screen that displays all pertinent times in hundredths of a second. Competition handgunners are principle users, but these devices lend themselves well to other shooting disciplines. They're lots of fun on reactive targets or speed-shooting drills.

Reactive targets: We looked at these in the training Chapter. Check out the steel or self-sealing spinners. They're lots of fun and fairly affordable. Be sure to read the cautions included with these targets. Some of the synthetic types can shoot back with low-velocity airgun projectiles, and BBs are completely off limits on steel. The latter will have a minimum distance listing that should be adhered to. Splatter is always a concern.

A set of regulation .22 rimfire steel targets intended for "Metallic Silhouette" competition from 25 – 100 yards. They're also loads of fun if set up for informal practice.

Suppressor (or silencer): You will need a fistful of money to own one of these fascinating devices. They aren't legal everywhere, so your first step should be to check. The next hurdle is some BATF paperwork, endorsement from a local law enforcement head, and $200 for a special federal permit. This is on top of the cost for the actual device, which may run $450 to $1,000. Due to the red tape, some patience will be needed as well. With subsonic .22 LR ammo, a suppressor will be very quiet indeed. The sound of the action working will be nearly as loud as the report. The device will need a way to mount to a rifle, which is typically accomplished with a 1/2x28-threaded muzzle. Zero may change upon attachment, and the "can's" diameter may obstruct iron sights. Regular maintenance is necessary, too. However, one device may cover different

This self-sealing rimfire squirrel spins when hit.

rifles, including a .17 HMR (a .22 model works). The NFA stamp must accompany the device and owner at all times. In my state, ownership is legal with the proper federal credentials, but hunting is illegal. Looking at the expense, red tape, and restrictions, .22 CB Caps or Shorts seem like an attractive alternative!

SUMMARY

The "Essentials" list will get you started. You can always add those extras that pique your interest later. There are plenty of goodies to help lighten your wallet!

Sources: It's often nice to get your hands on a potential new gadget. A well-stocked local gun shop can be a good source for not only accessories, but also solid advice. The larger sporting retailers like Cabela's and Bass Pro have large and diverse inventories. They also mail order, as do Bownell's Midway USA, Graf & Sons, Natchez, and Gander Mountain.

CHAPTER 13

CLEANING, MAINTENANCE and STORAGE

The second book in the *Survival Guns* series is titled *Shotguns: A Comprehensive Guide.* Among the guns in a collection geared towards survival use, a shotgun makes a logical first choice. An included cleaning and maintenance Chapter provides a list of useful gear and solvents. With apologies to those who sprung for that edition, some of the information is excerpted below. Why? Because much of the same equipment will work! No, you can't stuff a .73 caliber 12-gauge brush through a .22 caliber barrel, but the solvents and handheld brushes will work. Rimfires, particularly .22s, accumulate a hard deposit of fouling, much of which is lead. While you could eventually scrape most of it off, the right tools and solvents will make things a whole lot simpler. Periodic cleaning will not only ensure reliability, but will also extend the life of your rifle. Regardless of the technique, this process is best done somewhere other than in the kitchen!

SAFETY

First, the obvious: inspect your rifle carefully to ensure it is unloaded! Then do it again. *Move any live ammunition to some out-of-reach location*, and put on a set of safety or shooting glasses for protection from solvent splatter or flying springs. When the job is finished, be sure to wash up thoroughly. Lead exposure is no joke, and besides direct ingestion, residual lead can be inadvertently deposited on furniture, clothing, or vehicles. This is a real concern for anyone with kids.

CLEANING KITS

Those starting from scratch will need a cleaning kit of some sort. It needn't be elaborate, but should contain a rod, bore brush, patches, solvent, lubricant, and a few other minor items like a toothbrush and rag. Prepackaged kits are available to help solve a bit of head-scratching. They make a good starting point, but most will be equipped with jointed aluminum cleaning rods that disassemble into sections.

Although there is a place for them, I much prefer a one-piece system. The joints can pick up crud, which won't help your bore. Not that a .22 needs constant cleaning - it normally doesn't. That's part of the fun of owning one. Still, you'll need to clean out fouling that accumulates in the action, barrel, and magazine. Semi-autos tend to get shot a lot, and are notorious collectors of crud.

We should clean the barrel through the breech whenever possible to avoid accuracy-robbing muzzle damage. That isn't always possible with closed actions, such as Ruger's 10/22. In that case, check out the Otis pull-through systems. The rod is replaced with a nylon-coated coiled length of braided stainless wire that has threaded fittings on its ends. It's a portable system that can simply be uncoiled and pulled through a barrel. The rimfire kit includes a bore brush and patch holder, plus a small T-handle that attaches to the pulling end. Everything is stored in a very compact pouch, which should have value for anyone on the move.

*Flexible Bore Snakes permit field expedient bore care.
They're also nice traveling companions.*

*The Otis flexible pull-through system works well in
tight actions, permitting breech-to-muzzle cleaning.*

Flexible pull-through devices like the "Bore Snake" have become popular, too. A weighted end is dropped into the open breech and down through the barrel. After it exits the muzzle, it can be pulled through from that end as bristle and swab sections do their magic. It'll get dirty, but can be washed. A flexible system is another good alternative for those on the move, but it can't dislodge anything stuck in a barrel.

I don't work out of a commercial cleaning kit, *per se*. Instead, I just employ an accumulation of gear, along with the solvents listed in *Shotguns: A Comprehensive Guide*. Some items, like my one-piece rifle rods are way too long for emergency travel. The jointed rods see very little use, although a section may be used for handgun cleaning duties. The pull-through kit is a bit fiddly to use so it often sits idle in proximity to a collection of well-used rods. The Otis kit does see occasional use when breech-to-muzzle cleaning won't work. At other times, it remains in its pouch, providing a reassuring grab & go alternative.

Solvents & lubricants: Most of the items shown below are from *Shotguns: A Comprehensive Guide*. Consider them a home-based collection that will cover all likely needs. It won't take much to clean and maintain a rimfire rifle. Our firearms unit buys some of these products by the gallon. However, you could easily survive with just the first two items, which are available in very small containers.

Be sure to read their labels prior to application. Some readers will no doubt disagree with our choices, but after steady use for many years, we know they work:

Shooter's Choice: This is our go-to solvent. It doesn't have the aroma of Hoppe's, but it sure is hell on fouling of all kinds. It's worth applying a small test drop to an inconspicuous area, to make sure nothing dissolves. Many rimfires have plastic parts and synthetic stocks, some of which are film-dipped. So far, I haven't damaged anything, possibly because any errant drops are promptly cleaned off.

Breakfree CLP: We use it for general lubrication of metal-on-metal contact points. It also works well for final wiping of metal surfaces, and effectively inhibits corrosion. I've seen test results involving ferrous metal and salt baths, in which this product rated high. The military uses it for the same reason, and CLP stands for "cleaner, lubricant and preservative".

A collection of useful solvents and lubricants, as detailed below.

Rem Oil: It's general purpose gun oil, which can be used to lubricate action parts or wipe down exterior metal surfaces. A small bottle is always on hand.

Gun Scrubber: Sold in aerosol cans, this evaporative solvent is similar to break cleaner. It effectively cuts fouling in hard-to-reach areas, but it will leave parts bone dry. Be careful not to get any in your eyes or night-sight elements.

Rust Prevent: As a final step, we often spray on a film from an aerosol can. It soon dries, leaving a protective coating that won't attract debris. It smells good, too!

JB Bore Paste: This is one of those seldom-used items that can prove invaluable at times. It's a very mild abrasive paste that cuts stubborn barrel fouling. Just clean normally, and then run a JB-impregnated patch through the bore. You'll probably be surprised by the amount of crud that comes out. I only use it on a very dirty barrel, taking care to flush it out afterwards with a solvent-soaked patch.

Rods, patches, and brushes: The list may look a bit imposing, but don't forget that many of the items can be used with airguns as well as other firearms. Note the emphasis on one-piece cleaning rods. You may want to add a separate pull-through system as well. It won't occupy much space and can be augmented with a few jury-rigged extras. The following items will provide a useful home-based inventory of gear:

Rods: You may wind up buying a self-contained cleaning kit, *and* a separate one-piece rod. Those designed for .17 caliber barrels will be very flexible due to their small diameters. Put much pressure on one and it may spring at mid-length, tapping the bore. A nylon-coated rod is therefore a wise investment. For bores of .22 caliber or greater I still like a one-piece stainless rod, mainly because its surface can't trap imbedded particles. A pull-through kit will prove useful for folks who can't clean from breech to muzzle.

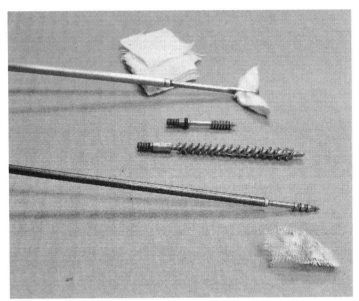

One-piece rods with patch retaining options and a .22 bore brush. The small diameter .17 rod is nylon coated. Its patch jag works okay with half of a .22 patch.

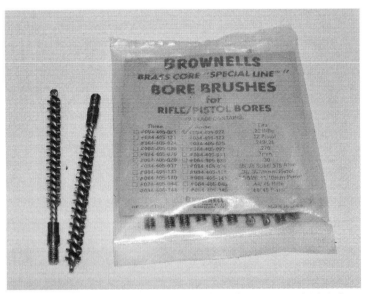

Brownell's "Special Line" brushes employ a brass core which is less likely to damage the delicate rifling in small-bore barrels.

Bore brushes: We use Brownell's "Brass Core Special Line Brushes" in appropriate calibers. After contact with solvent, flush them with Gun Scrubber to wash off any copper-eating chemicals.

Patch holders: Slotted tips are standard in most kits. The brass versions are less likely to cause bore damage. They'll work, but for better results, I like a jag as well. It's a little caliber-specific brass drum with an O-ring guide, and a pointed tip that helps to center a patch. With the correct patch size, it will squeeze through the barrel, providing uniform patch contact, for improved cleaning.

Patches: You'll need some .22 patches (they can be cut in half for use in .17 barrels). I use GI M16 patches that always seem to be on hand. They're roughly 1 ¼-inch square. They are a bit thick for use with a jag, but they can be sized down by pulling a few loose strands off of the edges.

M16 toothbrush: Picture a toothbrush with an extra set of small bristles on its handle. It's good for brushing out small spaces like the actions of .22 semi-autos. Or just use a regular toothbrush. Don't mix it up!

Stainless steel toothbrush: These are heavy-duty toothbrushes with thick black plastic handles and stiff metal bristles. They'll really cut through heavy fouling when used with Shooter's Choice. However, they need to be used with caution. A disassembled bolt *may* get some careful brushing on its heavily fouled face, while avoiding the extractor. Any muzzle scrubbing is out!

Cotton swabs: They permit access to tight spots like extractor cuts. Q-tips will do the same job but the longer, wood-shaft medical types are a bit handier.

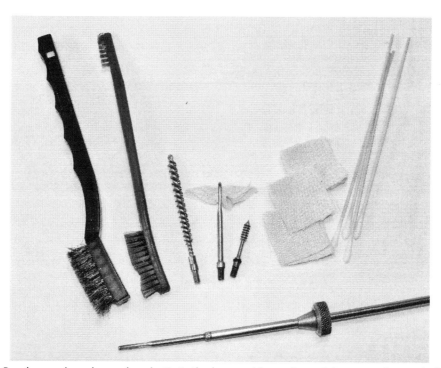

Brushes and swabs are handy. So is the bore guide on the stainless one-piece rod. If used carefully, it can prevent barrel crown damage.

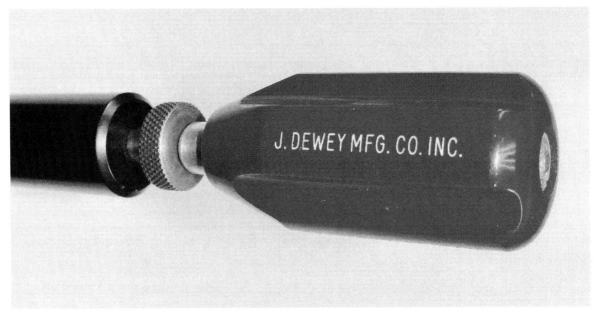

When breech-to-muzzle cleaning isn't practical a brass bore guide helps maintain a centered cleaning rod.

CLEANING

I'll seldom fire more than 20 rounds through a prized centerfire rifle without a thorough cleaning. On the other hand, a pet .22 rimfire may not see any detailed service for several hundred rounds. A good example is my custom Ruger 10/22. Its solid receiver won't accept a rod, and disassembly is somewhat of a project. Instead, I just brush out the receiver area as best I can after a few boxes of ammo. The magazines get the same treatment. After a couple of bricks have been fired, the stock will come off so the bolt can be removed for detailed service. Plenty of hard, gray fouling will be evident in that area. The two pins capturing the trigger assembly can be pushed out for cleaning of unburned powder flakes and debris. The barrel can then be cleaned using a pull-through system.

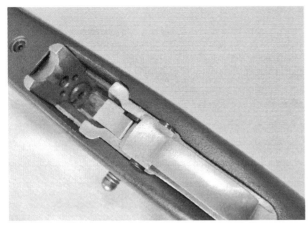

Ruger 10/22 ready for stock removal. The safety button must be carefully centered to clear the stock. Note the empty chamber.

Ruger 10/22 barreled action removed from its stock.

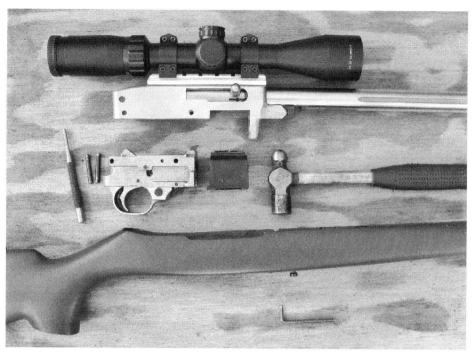

Ruger 10/22 in the process of detailed cleaning. The bolt still needs to come out, which requires driving out the buffer pin located on the receiver's upper rear.

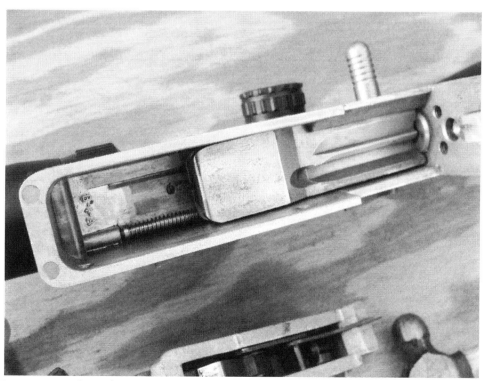

Bottom view of a 10/22 receiver and bolt. The aftermarket synthetic buffer must be removed in order to draw the bolt fully rearward. At that point it can be separated from the bolt-handle and spring guide for removal. It's a bit "fiddly", even if you hold your mouth just right.

My bolt guns tend to see more frequent cleaning due to their ease of disassembly. It only takes a few seconds to remove the bolt for direct access to the receiver and barrel.

Many .22 bolt-action rifles require holding the trigger rearward while withdrawing the bolt. This one has a convenient separate bolt release.

Unlike some of the hot rock small-bore centerfire calibers, rimfire barrel cleaning is often fairly simple. Severe copper fouling shouldn't be an issue (except maybe for the new .17 Winchester Super Magnum), so a few passes with solvent-moistened patches may clean a barrel that hasn't been neglected. In fact, some experienced shooters seldom clean their .22 rimfire rifle bores. They often stick with one well-tested target load. Most such projectiles are made out of relatively soft lead, which won't excessively wear the rifling. Their belief is that the barrel will only foul to a certain point, filling in its minor imperfections with a uniform coating of lead. Many more .22 rimfire fans switch loads, depending on availability and cost. Those using rimfire Magnums will be

A bolt-action is easy to service. It only takes a few minutes to clean its face and extractors.

firing plated or jacketed bullets, so some copper-fouling may accumulate. In such cases, a bore brush will be called for along with a bit more elbow grease.

At some point, *every* rimfire rifle will need attention. It's a machine with metal parts that need to run freely on lubricated surfaces! The most ignored rimfire rifles are semi-automatics. We've seen some that were true nightmares. They looked okay from the outside, but evil forces lurked within. Unlike centerfire semi-automatics, most rimfires are blowback operated. They lack the extra parts associated with a gas-operated system, which makes cleaning a bit simpler. However, like other repeating rimfire designs, they do accumulate fouling within their receivers. If ignored, it will build up until the rifle's function is impaired. At some point, a seized firing pin or heavily fouled breech face could result in an out-of-battery discharge. That's both exciting and dangerous! You *will* need to take your rifle apart occasionally to clean out the hard deposits of lead and burned powder.

A coin will get you inside a Marlin Model 39 lever-action rifle.

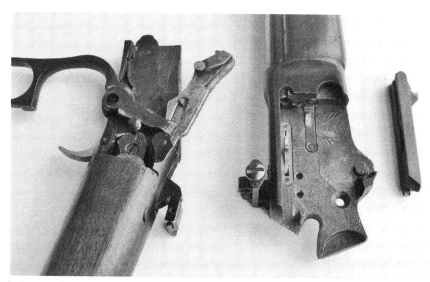

The Marlin's two-piece receiver separates for easy maintenance and breech-to-muzzle bore cleaning.

There is usually some way to remove the bolt for proper cleaning. A lever-action Marlin M39 may look daunting, but it can actually be disassembled without much difficulty. Loosening the take-down screw permits separation of the receiver halves. At that point, the bolt can be withdrawn for direct access to the breech. Most bolt-action rifles have easily removable bolts. There may be separate release, or the trigger may just need to be held to the rear (sometimes, both). S&W's semi-automatic rimfire AR disassembles like an M16 for easy bolt removal. Others, like the Ruger or Marlin, require more effort. Thanks to modern technology, it's usually easy enough to locate an owner's manual. Once an appropriate plan of attack is formulated, it's time to go to work…

S&W's M&P 15-22 is a breeze to clean. It breaks open like an AR-15 but lacks the more complicated gas system.

Barrel: Again, cleaning from the breech end is generally the best approach. Fouling won't be as likely to enter the action, and damage to the barrel's crown will be prevented. To reiterate, the pull-through systems are the best solution for guns that won't accommodate a rod.

I may clean a non-match grade barrel through its muzzle, using a rod. A Remington Model 572 pump is a good example. It will provide useful field-grade accuracy, but is unlikely to appear in any Olympic events. Mainly to save time, I'll clean a rifle of this type through the front end while proceeding with care. You can degrade accuracy not only through neglect, but also by careless cleaning. Regardless of the actual barrel cleaning tool, the procedures remain similar.

Step #1: I'll usually start with a patch on a slotted tip that's been sprayed with a shot of Gun Scrubber, using just one pass. The patch is discarded after it exits the muzzle. It'll pick up any grease coatings or debris to help make the next steps easier.

Step #2: A solvent-soaked bronze brush is passed through the barrel while taking care to maintain a centered rod (we use Shooter's Choice). The brush should fit snugly, but it should not require excessive force. Accuracy of the best-shooting rifles can be maintained by unscrewing the brush every time it emerges from the muzzle. At that point, the rod can be withdrawn and wiped off. This is easier on a good barrel than running the brush back and forth with accumulated fouling. In all cases, make sure the brush exits the barrel before reversing direction! Depending on how many rounds have been fired, you may need as few as three or four passes, or possibly a dozen or more. Take care to prevent solvent from running throughout the action and stock.

Note: Some knowledgeable accuracy freaks substitute a solvent-saturated patch for a brush.

Step #3: Swap the brush for a well-fitting patch, attached to either a loop or jag. The first patch should turn into a mess! The second should look a bit better. Keep going until the patches begin to come out clean. They probably won't be spotless, but they should show only minimal discoloration.

Step #4: Depending on the duration of storage, an oiled patch can be passed through the bore to prevent corrosion. In that case, run a clean patch through the barrel before it is fired (it's a good idea to check for a clear bore, too). So far, thanks to a stable storage environment, I haven't found this last step necessary.

Note: If the barrel seems excessively fouled, it might be time to break out the JB Paste. Read the directions and repeat Step #3, afterwards.

Once the barrel is cleaned, don't forget to flush solvent off the bronze bore brush, using a shot of Gun Scrubber.

Action: An M16 toothbrush with some solvent should handle the hard fouling that accumulates on the receiver, bolt face, and breech. That stainless toothbrush may come in handy, but proceed with caution! Make sure the extractor moves freely and is cleared of any fouling. Trigger groups should receive periodic attention, and Gun Scrubber is sometimes a good way to flush out powder residue. Apply a couple drops of Breakfree or Rem Oil to the firearm's moving parts afterwards, and then cycle the action a few times.

Magazines: Springs and followers should be periodically cleaned. The tubular types can be cleaned as a barrel, using a patch on a rod. Some people skip this step, which can create a real safety hazard. The day may come when a live round hangs up inside a tubular magazine that hasn't been maintained! Before disassembling any detachable magazines, it's worth keeping a spare on hand to use as a reference during reassembly. Mostly, I just flush them out with Gun Scrubber. Oily magazines will just attract dirt, resulting in stoppages. Some lubes, like WD-40, will also kill primers.

Exterior: The last step involves applying a protective layer of oil to the metal exterior. You can wipe on a thin film of Breakfree or Rem Oil, or spray on a light layer of Rust Prevent. Watch out for your optics, though! Scope rings and metal magazines can be lightly wiped afterwards with the same cloth.

Scope: A set of lens caps are a wise investment. They'll not only ward off water or dust, but also solvents and oils. The best way to clean the lenses is to blow them off. That won't always work, so a "Lens Pen" is a wise investment. You *can* clean a lens with caution by misting its surface with a breath, followed by gentle attention and a very soft cleaning patch or eyeglass cloth. Just remember that the special anti-reflective coatings are very thin. Don't mess with any screws in the scope. It's a sealed unit, and disassembly will ruin it.

STORAGE

The following excerpt from *Shotguns: A Comprehensive Guide* applies equally well to other firearms, as well as airguns:

"Periodic inspections and basic cleanings go a long way towards peace of mind, and will also help maintain your investment. The means of storage is equally important. External corrosion can appear in a surprisingly short amount of time and, if undiscovered, it can cause pitting and permanent damage. Long-term gun case storage may result in transfer of moisture from padded surfaces, which can accumulate humidity. Believe it or not, sometimes the moisture can appear in minutes. We've seen firearms literally covered in water droplets after their soft cases were exposed to intense sunlight. These guns were properly stored at home and cased for a trip to the range. The soft interiors had probably absorbed moisture over time, and upon arrival, the cases were placed in the sun. Soon afterwards, their interiors turned into saunas, causing "sweating" that condensed on the guns. It happened to me, and a fast wipedown saved the day. The case was spread open to dry in the sun. If, for some reason, the gun had remained in the case for a while, things would have turned out differently.

A gun safe offers peace of mind as well as security.

The same situation can occur in reverse, upon entering a warm area from low temperatures. Moisture will quickly condense on a cold firearm, covering it with water droplets. Those spending time in remote winter locations often leave their working gun outdoors for this reason. A gradual warmup with constant attention is otherwise necessary.

Besides gun cases, wrapping a gun in cloth can wreak havoc, even if stored indoors. Any damp place like a basement or shed is just as bad, but long-term vehicle storage can cause similar problems. Ammunition is also best stored in a cool, dry location. It will last for decades with care, whereas heat will cause rapid deterioration. Moisture is as bad for ammo as it is for guns!

That's why a good gun safe located in a dry and stable environment is worthwhile. Desiccant packs and dehumidifier rods should provide adequate protection from rust if some thought goes into the final location. I haven't had any issues using a safe alone, which is located in a primary living space.

The extra peace of mind afforded by a good safe is another major dividend. The *Survival Guns* edition covers safes and other storage options in detail. We all have an obligation to ensure that our firearms and ammunition don't fall into the wrong hands. A locked case or trigger lock may deter kids or honest folks but are really just interim steps."

Springs & storage: During long-term storage, we prefer to relax the tension on a few key springs. Opening the action will typically cock a hammer or striker, which is normally powered by a strong coil spring. A semi-auto also has a recoil spring that undergoes compression while its bolt is locked rearward. On a range, a shoulder-fired gun should be placed in a vertical rack that way for safety's sake. It'll be fine short-term, but don't store a semi-auto on a long-term basis in that condition. A weakened recoil spring will degrade function, and could cause damage to the gun from excessive bolt velocity.

Dry-firing a rimfire is not advised. It's actually okay to do so with some types that are specifically designed for this purpose, but overall, you run the risk of denting the chamber mouth. At that point you'll get misfires or stoppages. Here are a few options:

Bolt-actions can usually be un-cocked by lifting the handle and squeezing the trigger as the bolt is slowly eased downward. The same basic idea will, of course, apply to any hammer guns. Sometimes semi-auto dry-fire damage can be minimized by ever-so-slightly retracting the bolt, and holding it while the trigger is pulled. The internal hammer or striker may release without full firing pin/breech contact. Or you can buy a snap cap designed for this purpose.

Note: Whatever technique is employed, please make darned sure the gun is unloaded! Then, store it responsibly.

Sources: Brownell's and Midway USA catalog a large selection of gun cleaning gear and solvents. In addition to their catalog, Cabela's has a number of walk-in retail locations for some hands-on shopping. Your local gun shop is worth a visit as well. Since some also provide gunsmith service, a good customer relationship can prove valuable.

CHAPTER 14

CONCLUSION

Much like any other well-equipped tradesman, I'd like a number of good tools in my kit. If all should happen to function similarly, then so much the better. The use of one will reinforce skills with the others. Competent operation and accurate shooting help!

A logical starting point is a rifle chambered in .22 Long Rifle. Although prices have risen, you can still shoot one without going broke. Although .22 LR rounds remain scarce, the odds are better of locating at least *some* ammo. Don't forget that .22 Shorts or Longs will also fire in a Long Rifle chamber. The various specialty types like CB Caps offer further possibilities for ultra-quiet hunting or close-range pest control. With such loads, you really can turn your rimfire rifle into a surrogate "airgun". The training aspect shouldn't be overlooked either. In a pinch, with the right cartridges, your .22 LR may further serve for self-defense. Granted, a centerfire choice would be a better bet. Through careful shopping, you could also match a rimfire version to a larger centerfire rifle, thereby reinforcing competency with both firearms. As for stocking the larder, I'd consider the .22 LR's ethical cutoff point to be raccoon-sized animals, preferably with head shots. Plenty of deer have been poached with garden-variety .22 Long Rifle bullets, but many have also been lost. Such a stunt would need to be confined strictly to survival circumstances, and only then with a carefully placed shot to the head. No doubt about it - a good old-fashioned .22 caliber rimfire rifle is one darned useful firearm!

Those looking for more punch may be well served by a .22 Magnum rifle. Ammunition cost will be higher, but not still not out of line. You'll likely forego the training aspect. But, when used to tackle animals, 50 cartridges should last a long time, and a box will easily slip in a pocket. The .22 WMR is a quantum leap in power above a .22 LR, which comes with some increase in noise. Still, the report is much lower than a .223, and less meat will be damaged. Defensively, the .22 Winchester Magnum Rimfire will be less of a stopper, but still a whole lot better than any .22 LR. Afield, the higher velocity of the .22 WMR will flatten its trajectory and increase practical range by at least 50 yards, out to somewhere around 125 paces. Terminal effect on game will be noticeably improved as well. Animals as large as eastern coyotes could be harvested with careful shooting. In my home state, the .22 Magnum is legal for deer, but that's really a stretch. I'd want a perfect shot at relatively close range to the neck or brain. Small game meat damage could be minimized through the same technique, or by switching to a full metal jacket bullet.

A .17 Hornady Magnum Rimfire will offer interesting possibilities for some folks, most of whom will probably be into shooting. Since it is based on a .22 Magnum cartridge, noise will be similar. However, the necked down brass is geared toward tiny flyweight bullets launched at much higher velocity. Bullet expansion will be dramatic, and its small mass will likely result in near total disintegration. One great trait the .17 HMR offers is predictably excellent accuracy, although the light bullets are greatly affected by wind. All things considered, the .17 HMR is really more of a specialty cartridge. It's my favorite rimfire load, but in reality, it remains primarily a varmint choice for use on animals like crows or prairie dogs, at ranges out to 150 yards. I'd tackle a fox with the .17 HMR, and even a coyote with a careful headshot. Anything bigger would be a last-ditch effort requiring careful bullet placement with uncertain results.

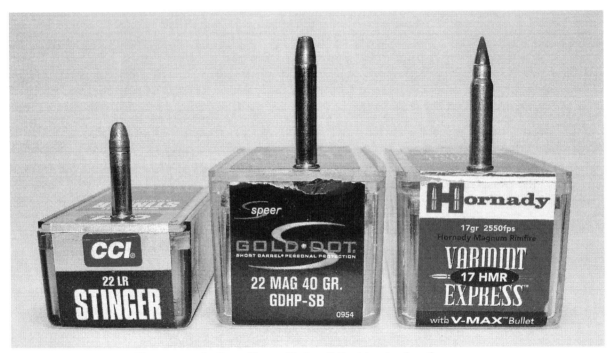

Three great rimfire calibers offering distinct levels of performance.

As for the other rimfire choices like the 5mm, .17 Mach 2, or new .17 Winchester Super Mag, for survival purposes, we should consider them as novelties. Stick with the mainstream choices, and you'll be better off.

Living with only one rimfire would be tough, but it could be a financial or logistics-driven reality for some of us. If forced to make a choice my pick would be a rifle chambered in .22 LR. The power of the hotter Magnums would be exchanged for the flexibility to use quiet .22 Shorts and CB Caps. People in this boat may be well-served with a Remington Model 572 .22 pump, which feeds just about everything. It would also complement the 12-gauge Model 870 pump shotgun, and .308 Model 7600 centerfire rifle detailed in *Survival Guns: A Beginner's Guide*. Others might opt for a .22 LR bolt-action, which can be hand-fed nearly any type of .22-cartridge. With the right rimfire ammunition, an airgun, although a worthwhile addition, would not be absolutely essential.

Three matching pump-action picks that can cover all bases: Remington's M-572 .22 Rimfire; M-7600 .308 centerfire; and M-870 12 Gauge shotgun.

Yes, a .22 LR is a great choice. Add a second rifle in .22 or .17 Magnum, and you'll have best of all worlds. We may also choose to add a low-impact airgun, but that's the subject of the next edition. Meanwhile, go out and enjoy your rimfires. As a way to put meat in the pot, or as an economical method to train, you can't go wrong.

OTHER *SURVIVAL GUNS* TITLES

If you purchase a gun safe and attempt to fill it up in one fell swoop, you'll be hemorrhaging dollar bills. To keep things manageable, why not adopt an incremental approach? That's exactly what's been done with the succession of firearms manuals. You can focus on just one system and chip away until the essentials have been procured. The old saying "a little knowledge is a dangerous thing" certainly holds true with firearms. Accordingly, each book serves as a source for in-depth knowledge pertinent to specific system. Furthermore, each is geared towards survival-based roles and the core principles espoused in *Survival Guns: A Beginner's Guide*.

SURVIVAL GUNS FIREARMS PUBLICATIONS IN PRINT

Survival Guns: A Beginner's Guide: This book is the first in the series, and serves as a guide to help build a basic firearm battery. It starts with a gun safe, to which firearms and accessories are added using a planned process. To help make the best choices, some key underlying principles are defined. From there, procurement of several essential systems can commence. A baseline inventory of a shotgun, two rifles, and a handgun serve as cornerstones. Further additions include some interesting specialty firearms and accessories. The firearms on the essentials list, as well as many other types, will be thoroughly covered in the series of system-specific manuals. In each, the various models, ammunition, and accessories will be closely examined. While this book is written for beginners, those familiar with firearms should find topics of value. The information will be detailed, covering far more than just a firearm itself.

Shotguns: A Comprehensive Guide: Would you like a bird gun, riot gun, and high-powered rifle all rolled into one single shotgun? Where's the tradeoff on recoil and performance? What shells work best with different chokes? This publication covers everything you ever wanted to know about shotguns. Technical aspects are explored, including the different types of guns, gauges, shells, chokes, shot sizes, and ballistics. Accessories are examined, along with training tips and other useful information. The human factor is addressed, with methods to accommodate smaller-statured shooters. Putting it all together, you'll not only have serious defensive capabilities, but also a means for the harvesting of both small game and very large animals. This shotgun manual shows you the way.

Air Rifles: A Buyer's and Shooter's Guide: Did you know that you can mail-order airguns in most locales? Unlike conventional firearms, they aren't federally regulated. They'll also get you into some tight places that would be strictly off limits to any powder-burning guns. The latest air-powered technologies are a quantum leap beyond a common BB gun, offering real quality and impressive performance. How about a rifle that runs on high-pressure air to combine effortless operation with multiple shots? These pre-charged types are filled from a scuba tank. Accuracy is phenomenal and so is power, yet noise is less than most silenced firearms. And again, no special BATF permits are necessary. Some can even be purchased as big-bore versions in .45 and .50 caliber. Others run independently from highly compressed springs or gas-strut type technologies. This publication provides the knowledge you'll need to fully exploit the advantages of these intriguing guns. A wide range of ammunition and powerplants are explored, along with their advantages and limitations. Scopes and other sighting systems are detailed, as are useful accessories. The airgun manual is your source for non-firearm technologies, from plinking and training through hunting.

FUTURE *SURVIVAL GUNS* PUBLICATIONS

The Centerfire Rifle/AR-15 Manual: Are you interested in leverguns or semi-auto rifles? How about bolt-actions, or an entire family of guns in different calibers? How do you choose the right scope, and how do you sight it in? How do you select the most accurate loads, or pick the right bullets? How do you reduce recoil for younger shooters? Following in the steps of *The Rimfire & Airgun Manual*, the centerfire book takes us to the next level. Optics and ballistic aiming systems are explored, along with skill-building regimens. You'll see methods to assess true accuracy, and other useful tips. Different calibers and loads are discussed, as are various rifle choices. The AR-15 has grown wildly popular, with dozens of brands and hundreds of accessories to choose from. It's an extremely versatile platform for good reason, and can be instantly transformed to many different profiles. Switch-top conversions are possible in .22 LR, through several pistol calibers, and serious big-bore rounds. On top of that, universal "Picatinny" mounting points will easily accommodate nearly unlimited optical or equipment choices. Since most of us don't have unlimited funds, we'll need to determine exactly *which* accessories are necessary. This edition is the next progression in our system-based approach for development of a practical firearms battery.

The Handgun Manual: You can shoot yourself with the wrong combination of pistol, holster and clothing, so which ones are dangerous? You may understand the fundamentals of shooting, but how do they apply to handguns? Are you interested in a 1911 pistol? If so, did you know you can create your own multi-caliber pistol off a single frame? What about other types? Which loads are your best defensive choices? This publication covers everything you'll need to know about handguns, from different models through practical calibers, holsters, and accessories. You'll see some interesting alternatives to six-shot revolvers and the latest high-capacity pistols. The smaller guns are covered, too. Practical revolver and pistol skills are detailed, along with recommended practice regimens. *The Handgun Manual* rolls all of this information into one source for safe and effective handling.

Printed in Great Britain
by Amazon